The Missing Ones

A Journey of Hope and Healing for
Families of Prodigals

The Missing Ones

A Journey of Hope and Healing for
Families of Prodigals

Written by Joy Morey

Foreword by Pastor Eric Lehmann

Fusion Publishing
Butler, PA

Copyright © 2021 by Joy Morey

Website: www.DiscoveringJoy.net

Email: TheMissingOnes@DiscoveringJoy.net

All rights reserved. No part of this publication may be reproduced, stored or transmitted in any form or by any means, electronic, mechanical, photocopying, recording, scanning, or otherwise without written permission from the publisher. It is illegal to copy this book, post it to a website, or distribute it by any other means without permission.

Unless indicated otherwise, all Scripture quotations are taken from The Holy Bible, New International Version® NIV® Copyright ©1973, 1978, 1984, 2011 by Biblica, Inc.® Used by permission. All rights reserved worldwide.

ISBN 978-1-7335626-8-3

Printed in the United States of America

Published by Fusion Publishing Group
Butler, Pennsylvania 16002

Dedicated with Love

To my Mom and Mom-in-Love:

your prayers move the heart of the Father

Table of Contents

Foreword by Pastor Eric Lehmann i

Introduction iii

1. **The Hopeful Heart:** Dealing with Relational Trauma 1
2. **The Heart of the Father:** Unending Love 9
3. **The Heart of the Prodigal:** Ripe for Deception 15
4. **The Hurting Heart:** Choosing to Forgive 21
5. **The Heart for the Prodigal:** Taking A Stand 27
6. **The Humble Heart:** Accepting Responsibility 41
7. **The Hungry Heart:** Pursuing Relationship 47
8. **The Healing Heart:** The Productive Process 51
9. **The Heart with Vision:** Speaking Life 61
10. **The Heart of Restoration:** New but Purposeful Normal 71
11. **The Homebound Heart:** The Repentant Prodigal 79
12. **The Heartbeat of God:** Filling the Gap 89
13. **The Hesitant Heart:** Letter of Hope for the Precious Prodigal 95

Appendix I: Music Resources 99

Appendix II: Helpful Links 102

Acknowledgments 103

Notes 105

Contact the Author 108

Foreword

By Pastor Eric Lehmann

There may be many reasons why you opened the pages of this book. You might be feeling the gut-wrenching pain of having been betrayed by someone close. You might have been abandoned and left alone. You might be struggling with seeing a family member make decisions that are painful to themselves and to those around them. You might be holding on to promises that God gave you and are standing in faith for the return of a loved one. You might want to learn more about how to reach out to those who are hurting and praying for their prodigal to come home. Well, it's not by accident that you were drawn to open this book.

What you are about to read will touch you, inspire you and encourage you. Joy Morey has a gift to paint a picture with her words. You will find yourself leaning into what she is saying, sitting back and reflecting, and then standing up in faith for a breakthrough. Anchored in Scripture and forged in the fire of experience, this book will bring healing, hope, and faith to your life and ministry.

My wife Sarah and I have known Joy and her family for over twenty years. She is one of the most kind, compassionate, and authentic people we have ever known. We have watched her walk out the pages of this book and we had the privilege of being a part of one of the most beautiful stories of restoration and healing that we have ever seen.

Joy writes from her heart with passion. I can assure you that every word and every sentence has been lived out in the real world of thoughts, emotions, and actions. I say that because what you are about to read is not just theory. These are principles that have been hammered out and tested by trial and suffering.

I believe that as you turn these pages, the Spirit of God will touch you, heal you, and motivate you. Faith is rising, even for "the missing ones."

Eric Lehmann
Senior Pastor at Freedom Church
Wesley Chapel, Florida

www.FreedomChurchWC.com
www.HealingtotheNations.com

Introduction

"As you mend, you move from needing help to giving help."[1]
- Suzanne Eller

The missing ones… those who should be sitting with you at the dinner table, working beside you in everyday chores, and walking with you on an evening stroll. These are the spouses, children, siblings, parents, and friends who one time were constants in our life but have chosen to walk away and pursue a different path. Jesus referred to this beloved child gone astray as the prodigal. No matter the circumstances, a loved one not in fellowship with the Lord leaves an empty place at the Kingdom table. They are the missing one! The heart of the Father longs to have His table full! It's time for us to embrace the missing ones.

Loving the prodigal in our life is a journey with many twists and turns. As I write this, I'm journeying too. I'm so glad you've joined me! Isn't it encouraging to know you're not alone? I don't have all the answers and my story is still unfolding. Though, I've journeyed through the process of reconciliation with a repentant prodigal, I'm still in the process of grieving on behalf of other loved ones who are continuing the prodigal walk (or run as the case may be!) My heart is heavy with the knowledge that the time is short and the need is great.

I can't say there's a foolproof method for bringing the prodigal home. But I can say that there are proven ways we can hinder the prodigal from returning to the loving arms of the Father. I know this; I've made some of those mistakes. But the picture is still unfolding and God is still on the move! He is so faithful!

My purpose in writing these thoughts is multi-fold:
- To give hope to the prodigal
- To give hope to the prodigal's family
- To inspire active prayers for the prodigal
- To bring healing and peace to the hurting heart
- To avoid being a hindrance in the return or healing of the prodigal
- To learn to embrace the prodigal whether repentant or not

Though this parable is familiar, and you probably could preach a sermon from it yourself, I'm including it here for your review:

[11] Jesus continued: "There was a man who had two sons. *[12]* The younger one said to his father, 'Father, give me my share of the estate.' So he divided his property between them.

[13] "Not long after that, the younger son got together all he had, set off for a distant country and there squandered his wealth in wild living. *[14]* After he had spent everything, there was a severe famine in that whole country, and he began to be in need. *[15]* So he went and hired himself out to a citizen of that country, who sent him to his fields to feed pigs. *[16]* He longed to fill his stomach with the pods that the pigs were eating, but no one gave him anything.

¹⁷ "When he came to his senses, he said, 'How many of my father's hired servants have food to spare, and here I am starving to death! ¹⁸ I will set out and go back to my father and say to him: Father, I have sinned against heaven and against you. ¹⁹ I am no longer worthy to be called your son; make me like one of your hired servants.' ²⁰ So he got up and went to his father.

"But while he was still a long way off, his father saw him and was filled with compassion for him; he ran to his son, threw his arms around him and kissed him.

²¹ "The son said to him, 'Father, I have sinned against heaven and against you. I am no longer worthy to be called your son.'

²² "But the father said to his servants, 'Quick! Bring the best robe and put it on him. Put a ring on his finger and sandals on his feet. ²³ Bring the fattened calf and kill it. Let's have a feast and celebrate. ²⁴ For this son of mine was dead and is alive again; he was lost and is found.' So they began to celebrate.

²⁵ "Meanwhile, the older son was in the field. When he came near the house, he heard music and dancing. ²⁶ So he called one of the servants and asked him what was going on. ²⁷ 'Your brother has come,' he replied, 'and your father has killed the fattened calf because he has him back safe and sound.'

²⁸ "The older brother became angry and refused to go in. So his father went out and pleaded with him. ²⁹ But he answered his father, 'Look! All these years I've been slaving for you and never disobeyed your orders. Yet you never gave me even a young goat so I could celebrate with my friends. ³⁰ But when this son of yours who has squandered your property with prostitutes comes home, you kill the fattened calf for him!'

³¹ "'My son,' the father said, 'you are always with me, and everything I have is yours. ³² But we had to celebrate and be glad, because this brother of yours was dead and is alive again; he was lost and is found'" (Luke 15:11-32 NIV).

Using this Book

The hungry heart may digest this book in a few sittings. However, this book can also be used as a devotional tool or Bible Study. Each chapter includes a focused discussion, a prayer on your behalf, Scriptures to activate your faith, questions to apply your learning, and a declaration or prayer you can speak aloud to the Lord. These are all tools to help you in your journey. Music is healing, so included in the appendix are songs that align with the themes of each chapter. I pray that the words in this book will bring life and hope! Your Creator and Designer has such an amazing plan for your life! May you see it come to pass more each day as you develop a deep intimacy with the Lover of your soul!

1

The Hopeful Heart:
Dealing with Relational Trauma

"Circumstances may appear to wreck our lives and God's plans, but God is not helpless among the ruins."[2]
- Eric Liddell

Imagine feeling intense pain in your foot. The burning pins-and-needles sensation is so uncomfortable; you reach down to massage the foot… a foot that isn't even there! You are experiencing phantom pains… the sense of pain in a limb that has been severed through surgery or traumatic injury.

The pain of a missing limb can be excruciating and inescapable. The pain of a missing loved one can feel no less real.

When our relationships experience a traumatic injury, we feel the repercussions in our body and soul. When that loss is due to a choice instead of death, the pain is compounded by feelings of abandonment, failure, and disillusionment. The roller coaster ride of relational ups and downs has left you drained and nauseous and you are ready for the ride to end. Yet, relationships are precious and worth fighting for, right? But at what cost?

The desire to hope and the fear of disappointment wage war in our hearts. We cling to any sign that a prodigal is turning their heart toward home. Conversely, we reel with disappointment each time that seedling of possibility is trampled by reality.

Let me speak life to your hopeful heart today! Your desire to see a prodigal restored reflects the Father's Heart! This beloved person, whether they deem themselves a prodigal or not, has a spiritual champion in you! II Peter 3:9 states: *"The Lord is not slow in keeping His promise, as some understand slowness. Instead He is patient with you, not wanting anyone to perish, but everyone to come to repentance."*

That verse is for you and me! God's desire is that we would come into alignment with His will and plan for our lives. He waits patiently for us to repent, literally turn back, to the embrace of God's hand and heart. When you stand believing for any person to come into relationship with the Father, you are declaring His Kingdom would come and His will would be done on earth as it is in Heaven. You just can't go wrong praying that way!

"Return to your fortress, you prisoners of hope; even now I announce that I will restore twice as much to you" (Zechariah 9:12).

Praying in alignment with God's will gives you and me every reason to hope. So, climb up into the fortress of faith and become a prisoner of hope! Refuse to give up or give in as you believe for your treasured spouse, sibling, child, cousin, friend, or parent to return to the loving arms of the Father. Watch the Lord restore double in ways that you haven't even imagined!

The Prodigal's Journey

Picture your wayward loved one sitting in the corner of the pigsty, back propped up against the wall, fingering a half-eaten cob of corn. They're reminiscing about the wild ride they've been on. They've had some fun times, right?

But, what's running through their mind now? It depends on how long he or she has been sitting there. Early on, they are contemplating how to regain the responsibility-free lifestyle without the needed money or resources. But the longer they sit there, the more realization sets in. The long-buried, heart-deep truths begin to surface. Eventually, the revelation comes… the prodigal realizes that they've messed up royally. The Bible refers to this transition in thinking as "coming to his (or her) senses" (Luke 15:17, II Timothy 2:25b-26). This beloved prodigal now begins to consider how safety, provision, and relationship can be restored to his or her broken life. There's a long journey ahead. This wayward one knows that they've violated trust and wounded hearts along the way. The question becomes: Will they choose to head "home" or stay "lost?"

The Biblical prodigal went to a far country to enjoy his whims without family nearby to judge or nag. "Far country" can simply be characterized by being out of God's will or plan. Additionally, "far country" signifies being out of healthy relationship. The prodigal has set him or herself upon a course of action that differs from their God-given destiny. They are out of healthy relationship with the Heavenly Father. Additionally, the prodigal is most likely out of healthy relationship with the ones in their life—those they had previously been committed to through friendship, blood, or vows.

Your precious "missing one" may be in the far country physically and emotionally, as well as spiritually. Or they may be living nearby, even down the hallway. Just as the prodigal's father looked for his return home, often there is a parent, sibling, spouse, or child who peeks out the front window each day with a hopeful heart to catch a glimpse of their errant loved one. You may even be looking in the eyes of your prodigal each day for a glimmer of hope that your prodigal is coming "home." Regardless of where your precious prodigal is residing or what stage of the journey they are in, the resulting relational and emotional separation continues to be a painful reality for you.

Why Do Hearts Wander?

In the early 1990s, Disney made a repentant prodigal into a popular hero. Simba was a young cub when he watched his father die and was made to believe that it was his fault. He took off out of fear and shame pursuing a carefree life where his greatest concern was what he would eat and how he would spend his day. As you follow the plotline of Disney's The Lion King, you see that Simba's Pride (responsibility) is being taken over by the antagonist, Scar. Simba battles with his desire to avoid the pain of returning home and the possibility of failing in his duties. He must choose between the carefree life and his destiny. Spoiler Alert: Simba eventually returns home to embrace the responsibility of being the King of the Pride and rescues his Kingdom.

Without too much effort, you can think of some other fictional characters, such as Pinocchio or Nemo, who have similarly gone astray because of selfish desires, deceptive offers, painful experiences, or misguided plans. We may never understand why the prodigal chooses to abandon responsibility and moral integrity in favor of a lifestyle of their own choosing. Regardless, the prodigal lifestyle is a self-centered one. That loved one is bent on pursuing what they think will make them happy, and in the process, he or she is abandoning right and/or responsible living. The Psalmist talked about people who commit themselves to a sinful course and do not reject what is wrong (Psalm 36:4). Once caught in the web of lies, it is difficult for the prodigal to see the reality of their situation or to admit the need for change. Sadly, not every prodigal story ends with a "they lived happily ever after" tagline.

But... God!

His love changes everything! There's no medical prescription to fix wounded hearts, families, relationships. You'd be hard-pressed to find fool-proof methods of bringing home errant loved ones. Determining a fixed rate of healing is likewise impossible. But there are actions that go a long way towards encouraging healing and restoration! Few families do not have "missing ones," family members who've turned to a lifestyle that is hurtful, self-centered, and destructive. You are not alone in your desire to see these loved ones racing into the loving arms of the Father.

My hope is that the Lord speaks to your heart as you read, giving you hope, revelation, and wisdom as you pray for and love on your prodigal!

My prayer for you

Thank You, Lord, for this reader! What a blessing it is that they are committed to the beloved wanderer in their lives! Thank You that we can pray in alignment with your Word and heart. Bless this brother or sister today. Strengthen their resolve, restore their hope, guard their tender heart, and lift their vision higher! Be their Comforter, I pray! In Jesus' Precious Name, Amen!

Activation and Application

Read:

- Ezekiel 36:22-27, Pray verses 24-27 inserting your loved one's name for the pronoun "you."
- Psalm 37:3-9

Consider:

- What do I believe about God's desire to restore? Does my understanding line up with His Word?
- What encouragement can I draw from Psalm 37 during this journey?

- Write down specific areas that you would like to see the Lord move in on your behalf. Read Philippians 4:6-7, then add to your list some blessings and give thanks for them.

Declaration:

Dear God, You are so faithful and trustworthy! Thank You that You've never abandoned me. You said You would never leave my side. I choose to believe that today. I choose to trust that Your plans and purposes will come to pass. I thank You that You've been patient with me and with my loved ones. Please give me a steadfast love, kind words and actions, and wisdom to do what You deem is best. Thank You, Heavenly Father for Your love! I choose to be a prisoner of hope!

2

The Heart of the Father: Unending Love

"Real joy isn't found in how you feel about life; it's found in knowing how God feels about you!"[3]
- Bob Hazlett

Paint this scene in your mind: Jesus, surrounded by "sinners," chatting, teaching, snacking, laughing…

"What do the sinners look like?" you may ask. It's hard to say, probably like you and me: average people, trying to understand the Kingdom of God and how it applies to our broken and scuffed up lives.

Now look beyond the group… there, to the Pharisees and Scribes. They were the "holy" people, the teachers and preachers who knew the law and demanded that everyone follow it to a T. See them whispering? Jesus didn't have to see them. He knew what was in their hearts: condemnation, judgment, and disdain for Jesus and His listeners. So,

Jesus decided to turn His attention to the self-righteous and tell them a few stories.

In Luke 15, Jesus introduces the Pharisees and us to several characters: A shepherd who lost a sheep, a woman who lost a coin, a father who lost his son. Each lost item had value to the person; value that inspired them to rejoice when the item was returned. The shepherd lost 1/100th of his herd, yet he left the 99 to search for the lost one. The woman lost 1/10th of her coins. But her dowry would have been incomplete, so she searched for the missing coin. The father lost one half of his heart. He could have searched far and wide to locate his son or he may well have known exactly where his "lost boy" was living. But this was different than a misled sheep or a rolling coin. The son had a will of his own and would need to choose to be found. As each character received back that which was lost, he or she called to friends and neighbors to celebrate with them, just as all Heaven celebrates when one sinner repents. The moral of Jesus' stories was most likely lost on the Pharisees and Scribes. But we dare not lose sight of it!

The prodigal or lost son is merely a character. Yet, he is you; he is me. If we're truthful with ourselves, there has been a time or two or ten in our lives when we've played the prodigal... be it for an hour, a day, a month, or even years. Regardless, at one time or another you and I have been there... wandering in the far country, away from the Father.

There are many truths that we can gain from this parable. But first and foremost, let your heart latch onto this one: The Heart of the Father is filled with intense, deep, abiding love for you! Daddy God loves YOU and ME unconditionally! It's so deep, so wide, so all-encompassing, that we truly cannot fathom the depth of His *agape* (unconditional) love for us. It's so awesomely amazing, that when we turn our rebellious hearts to Him, all Heaven sees the joy on His face and breaks out in celebration.... Yes!! Over you and over me!

God values His children! He calls us His special treasure.[a] He sees us as the apple of His eye.[b] We are precious in His sight.[c] He created us marvelously![d] He delights in you and me.[e] We are not slaves, but sons and daughters.[f] Our Dad says we are chosen, royal, holy, and special![g] How treasured I feel as I read these thoughts!

Now, think about the prodigal in your life... Is it your spouse? A precious child? A parent? A sibling? A dear friend? Your Heavenly Father has that same deep and wide, all-encompassing love for each and every prodigal! His love never runs out and there's plenty to go around! That love continually draws us to Himself.

As you read this book, embrace the knowledge that no matter how much you love the prodigal, the Father loves them more! He longingly reaches for them, whispers His love, and weeps over their separation from Him. Take comfort in that. Know that your desire to see the prodigal restored falls into line with the will of the Father. May His Kingdom come and His will be done on earth as it is in Heaven!

My prayer for you

Daddy, I pray right now that You would bring a supernatural revelation of Your deep love to the person reading these words! May Your Holy Spirit show them how precious they are to You! Thank You, Lord! Help them to grasp the truth that nothing can separate them from Your love.

Activation and Application

Read:

Romans 8:31-39. Spend some quiet moments in His presence allowing your Heavenly Father to pour His peace and love on you.

Now, read this same Scripture inserting the name of your loved ones where appropriate.

Consider:

- Do I relate to God as a child to a loving Father? Why or why not?
- Do I need healing in regards to a father figure in my life? (If so, read Romans 8:14-17 and ask the Lord to heal that area of your heart and enable you to embrace Him as your Loving Father.)

Declaration:

Lord, Thank You for Your deep love for me! I am thankful that You love _____* so much more than I possibly can. As much as I would like _____* to be restored to my family and me, they truly need to turn their hearts to You, the Savior of our souls! I pray that Your Spirit would work in powerful ways in each of our hearts. Help me to listen to Your voice, to speak Your words, and to be Your hands of love extended in every situation, especially to _____*. Thank you, Faithful Father!

(* insert your loved one's name)

[a] Deuteronomy 7:6, NKJV
[b] Zechariah 2:8
[c] Isaiah 43:4
[d] Psalm 139:14 NKJV
[e] Isaiah 62:3-4
[f] Galatians 4:6-7
[g] I Peter 2:9

3

The Heart of the Prodigal: Ripe for Deception

"Look back in forgiveness, forward in hope, down in compassion, and up with gratitude."[4]
- Zig Ziglar

Picture this in your mind: A young man pacing back and forth in his bedroom, arguing with his friend. "Yes, my father trusts me! Besides, I have everything I need here, why should I leave?"

Yet later, when his friend heads home and he lies down for the night, discontentment and temptation begin to brew in his heart. The insidious lies of the enemy begin to whisper through his bedroom. It will only be a matter of days or weeks until the young man decides he has had enough of working for his dad. He deserves more! And thus, begins his foray into the land of the lost, also known as the far country.

Was it the sense of adventure calling him? Was it the day-to-day monotony? Was it a feeling of being "not good enough?" Was it lustful desire? Was it anger at a perceived injustice? We can speculate, wonder, and ask; but we may never know what drives a prodigal to pursue pleasure over purposeful living.

Why do people, even believers, find themselves in places they never thought they'd be? If you were to ask one or ten or a hundred who have journeyed to the far country, out of God's will and plan, they will assure you that there were some lies that they chose to believe. If we are honest with ourselves, there are times that we've believed a few of those whispered falsehoods too.

The problem with deception is that... well... it's deceiving! We don't know when we are being deceived if we are not actively pursuing the Truth! Think of it this way: You are a cashier collecting payment from a customer. They hand you two $50 bills. How would you know if the bills were counterfeit? You won't know... if you are not determined to find out the truth of their worth. But since you are aware that false bills have been a problem; you either compare the bills with what you know identifies an authentic $50 bill or you pull out a currency pen that will indicate the true worth of the bill. Only pursuing truth will keep falsehoods at bay.

Just as with Eve, the enemy has a way of twisting truth and distorting our perception of it. God had warned Adam in Genesis 2:17 *"...but you must not eat from the tree of the knowledge of good and evil, for when you eat from it you will certainly die."* The serpent said to Eve, *"You will not certainly die, for God knows that when you eat from it your eyes will be opened, and you will be like God, knowing good and evil"*

(Genesis 3:4-5). That deceiver took truth (knowledge of good and evil) and mixed it with the lie (you will not surely die) and added in a healthy dose of false promises. How easy it is to become armchair coaches, wondering how foolish Eve must have been to believe the deception.

Deception can be more kindly called "rationalization" but that doesn't negate the insidiousness of the false truths… "God understands my actions. After all, Jesus was tempted too."
"God would want me to be happy."
"Well, the Bible isn't clear on whether or not this is a sin."
"I will repent when it's all said and done. God forgives all, right?" "I've been hurt! My actions are understandable."

Regardless of the name they are called, none of us are exempt from being bombarded by lies of the enemy. So, what makes the difference between identifying the whispered ideas as lies or entertaining them as possible "truths?"

There are specific steps that can be taken to identify authentic truths from counterfeit ones. These steps are rooted in relationship with THE Truth. This Truth-verifying relationship is not just a one time, I've-been-saved-from-Hell experience, but an ongoing relationship that we invest in each day. These relationship steps include:

- **Know the Word of God:** Pursue truth through regular reading, meditation, and memorizing of the Scriptures. Psalm 119:11
- **Know the Love of God:** Develop an abiding understanding that God loves you and I so much that He has plans to prosper us. Trust in His plans. Jeremiah 29:11

- **Know the Voice of the Holy Spirit:** Interacting (listening and talking) with the Lord each day will enable you to identify His voice more readily. I Thessalonians 5:16-22
- **Know and be known:** allow authentic relationships with other believers to be a valuable part of your life. An authentic relationship involves honesty, trustworthiness, and love. It is this kind of friend that will help us identify areas of our life where we are believing lies; if we value their input more than our own current feelings. Proverbs 27:17

Consider this: If the young man in the parable had a healthy relationship with his dad, do you think he would have been as likely to abandon his home and squander his inheritance? If a believer has daily conversations with his/her Heavenly Father, do you think that he/she will be as easily deceived? I believe that we can confidently answer both questions with a "no."

Your prodigal has made some choices. Most likely those choices have been hurtful, costly, destructive, and even out of character. If you were to ask any prodigal "why" they made those choices, you'd probably see their shoulder shrug and hear a myriad of rationalizations for their behavior. Don't bother asking… the bottom line is that they have been deceived. Knowing this, you can confidently pray for God's revelatory power to invade their lives and hearts. Only His Truth can set the captive free! John 8:31-36

My prayer for you

Daddy, I lift up this precious reader to you! Thank You that Your mercies are new every morning! Today, may this reader hunger and thirst for Your truth like never before. Stir up the Holy Spirit in him/her to be the supernatural Lie-Detector so that he/she would not walk in deception. May they know Your Truth and walk in its freedom. Bring authentic relationships in their lives for encouragement and accountability. Thank You, Lord!

Activation and Application

Read:

- Hebrews 4:12, Allow the Lord to direct you to a verse to memorize for encouragement!
- Philippians 1:9-11

Consider:

- In what areas have I believed the enemy's lies? Lord, please show me!
- Use a concordance or online resource to search the Word of God for Truth to replace the lies that the Lord reveals to you! Seek input and prayer support from a trusted friend if needed.

Declaration:

Lord, Your Word says that You are the Way, the Truth, and the Life! Help me to learn Your Word so deeply that it would direct me towards Truth in every situation and relationship. I pray that my loved one will also come to their senses and discern Your Truth from the lies of the enemy! I know Your desire is that none should perish and I pray in agreement with Your heart today! Thank You, Father!

4

The Hurting Heart: Choosing to Forgive

"Forgiveness is not the absence of pain, but the presence of mercy."[5]
- Kris Vallotton

It takes no stretch of the imagination to picture an infected, oozing sore that won't seem to heal. You probably remember one you've had to nurse on yourself or another. Skin infections consistently have a few distasteful symptoms: oozing puss, stench, and pain! Any medical professional will inform the infection-bearing individual of the dire need to clean the wound and keep it that way! Antibiotics may even be necessary. Refusing to admit you have an infection will not cause the infection to go away! In fact, the opposite occurs… the infection grows and leads to amputation and/or death.

Your emotional and relational wounds need similar care. The effects of a once important, now broken, relationship need to be acknowledged and addressed. They require the thorough cleaning only found through laying the pain before the Lord and tapping into His supernatural power to forgive. This will most likely be a daily process as you exercise the choice to forgive over your hurting heart.

I say "choice to forgive" because when we are in emotional turmoil and heart-heavy pain, we don't really want to let the perpetrator off the hook by forgiving them! After all, they sure don't deserve that forgiveness and it's only right that they should experience pain like we are, right?!

I get it… I've been there. But staying there will lead to oozing hostility bringing the stench of sullenness and of course, perpetual pain.

You've most likely heard a variation of this popular phrase: Holding resentment is like drinking a poison and hoping it will kill someone else. Choosing to harbor anger and bitterness will cause you more pain and "infection" than it causes the one who hurt you. It will bring amputation and death to the current healthy relationships in your life.

Forgiveness is vital on multiple levels! One of the keys to understanding the Kingdom of God is realizing that forgiveness plays a crucial part in our relationships. It is so fundamental, that in Matthew 6:12 & 15 and in Mark 11:25, Jesus said that to gain forgiveness for ourselves, we must first extend forgiveness to others! Not just once… but many times! Why? Because unforgiveness is a poison that will creep into every aspect of your life. It will color how you perceive others; it will interfere with your trust levels; it will wreak havoc on your health; it will separate you from your loving Heavenly Father.

Aside from the pain, the greatest challenge of forgiveness is the reality of what it says. Forgiveness declares (in your heart) "I will no longer hold this person's actions against them or hope for them to get what they deserve." It is closing and shredding the file of the wrongdoer! Seems impossible, doesn't it? But that's exactly what God did for us! He shredded our transgression file and rewrote our history when He chose to forgive us!

Understand that releasing forgiveness does not condone the choices of the prodigal. It also does not erase the mess their behavior created. What it does is set you up for success in your relationships… with the Father, with others, and with the prodigal. It keeps clear the avenue of love so that you can reach out to them when the Lord provides opportunities.

Failure is Not an Option

When you come to grips with the truth of how destructive unforgiveness is, you realize that failing to forgive is not an option. Yet, it still seems to be an insurmountable feat. It generally is… if you are trying to do it on your own. But you are not alone! You have a Supernatural Coach who comes alongside you!

I appreciate this phrase a valued friend of mine uses: "Ask the Lord to put His 'super' on your 'natural!'" We're accountable for what we can do in the natural… which is always limited. But then, when we lay our feeble attempts at His feet, submitting to His will and ways, He puts His "super" on our humble beginnings! Forgiveness is one of those supernatural miracles that we can take part in. Let that stir up excitement and hope in your heart! God will do a work in and through you! His desire is to see you whole… walking in relationships where nothing is missing or broken. He longs to see you set free from unforgiveness and eventually from the pain of broken relationships.

But It Really Hurts!

When a loved one chooses prodigal living, they are casting aside the blessings, benefits, and affection of those who love them deeply. In the process of running towards self-fulfillment, most prodigals trample and crush some precious things. You, my dear reader, know this! Your heart has been bruised by the choices of the prodigal. You may have beautiful children, grandchildren, nieces, nephews, or siblings who show daily signs of being deeply wounded. Sometimes, the pain is exacerbated by new offenses on a consistent basis. You wonder how much more you can take or even why you should take it.

Hold tight! Feel the Father's tears mingle with yours as you reach up for His everlasting arms. Psalm 34:18 comforts us: "If your heart is broken, you'll find God right there; if you're kicked in the gut, He'll help you catch your breath" (Psalm 34:18 MSG). This situation has kicked you in the gut, but you are not alone and you will come through this!

Start today… don't worry about tomorrow, next week, or six months from now. Today, choose to forgive the one who abandoned you, choose to forgive the one who abused your kindness, choose to forgive the one who blames you, choose to forgive the one who trampled your heart, and… choose to forgive yourself if needed. You don't have to feel it to say it… push past the hurt, anger, and pain to speak the words in faith. Your faith put into action releases power in the spirit realm! His grace goes into action on your behalf! Stand firm! Watch, wait, pray, believe! Forgiveness will come… Your heart will heal!

Not only will you come through this… but when you turn your tear-stained face to Him and grab ahold of His hand… you'll emerge from this journey shining like gold! We have a choice, you and I. We can stay in our righteous indignation, anger, bitterness, and hurt. After all, the choices of others have been painful for us! Your Father knows this and understands. But, how much better it is to choose forgiveness and peace… to live freely with the knowledge that we are loved by the Father and He is so glad we are walking with Him!

My prayer for you

Dear Father, I pray right now for this precious reader. Only You know the depth of their hurt. Go deep, I pray, to the wounded places in their heart. Apply Your healing balm to soothe the pain. Be everything they need today, filling up all the empty places. Fill them with faith that You love them and the prodigal in their life. Restore Your joy to them despite the current circumstances! Thank You for being a faithful God!

Activation and Application

Read:

- Isaiah 43:1-7
- I John 2:3-11

Consider:

- Are there other people in my life besides the prodigal that I need to forgive? (Ask the Lord to bring those people to mind as you sit quietly.)
- Do I need to forgive myself for poor choices I've made?
- Have I held anger towards the Lord for not working things out the way I wanted?

Say these words out loud:
"Lord, with your help, I choose to forgive _____." Say it whenever the enemy reminds you of what this person did to you. Build onto this statement, when and as the Lord directs.

Declaration:

Dear Loving Father, I submit myself to You today! I act in faith, choosing to forgive even though I may not feel it in my heart. I declare that I will forgive others so that there will be nothing between You and me. Thank You for forgiving me even though I don't deserve it! Please let Your grace and love flow through me into all the relationships in my life… even the painful ones. I ask You to put your "super" on my "natural" so that I can see Your supernatural forgiveness and healing in my life and in my family. Thank You, Lord! I love You!

5

The Heart for the Prodigal: Taking A Stand

"Gratitude isn't only a celebration when good things happen. Gratitude's a declaration that God is good no matter what happens."[6]
- Ann Voskamp

Wallow with me for a minute in the pigsty of failure. Smell the stench of a time when your choices brought on pain and disappointment. Not exactly good memories, are they? It's a rough feeling to know that your mistakes have hurt others or wreaked havoc in your life.

Be careful of the pride that says, "I've never caused the kind of pain I'm walking through!" Sin is sin… consequences differ, but in the eyes of the Lord… sin is still sin. Your pigsty moment might be different than mine and different than the prodigal's, but the stench? It is the same.

At times, we all have run off to gad about in the meadows of sin, blatantly disregarding the incredible blessing of living in fellowship with Him. But when we turn our repentant eyes towards home, our hearts yearn for and anticipate the freedom found in restoration! I am so thankful that the Father's love for me pushes past the filthiness of the pig sty, the stench of poor choices, the rags of selfishness, and sees the purity of a repentant heart. He stands up to the accuser of the brethren and defends us as being righteous through His blood! What an awesome Heavenly Dad we have!! His forgiveness is rich! It is cleansing and healing! Oh, that each prodigal would step towards His loving, open arms! If our missing ones would only realize what lies in store for them… restoration, healing, freedom!

They may never admit it… but tucked away in the prodigal's heart is the hope that they are still loved; that there is still someone waiting in expectancy for their return. Mixed with that hope is an enemy-inspired fear that they will never find love and acceptance again. More than that, they may believe that they are beyond the Father's love and forgiveness.

Having Done All Else, Stand

It's been said that if you don't stand for something, you'll fall for anything. At some point in your current journey, you've decided that standing for your prodigal is a worthwhile endeavor. According to Isaiah 32:8, noble people make noble plans and stand for noble deeds. Believing for the healing and restoration of your precious loved one counts as a noble plan! When your confidence is in the Lord and His ways, your stand is a noble one!

The way you choose to stand is important. Standing is not a passive activity. Standing involves confidence, steadfastness, and readiness. In Ephesians 6, Paul equated the "stand" to the ready stance of a warrior. He understood what is needed to stand nobly and successfully! *"Therefore, put on the complete armor of God, so that you will be able to [successfully] resist and stand your ground in the evil day [of danger], and having done everything [that the crisis demands], to stand firm [in your place, fully prepared, immovable, victorious]"* (Ephesians 6:13 AMP).

Why Dress for Battle Only to Stand?

Don't underestimate the power of the stand! This is no typical battle! Our enemy does not follow the rules; he does not come at us in obvious, typical ways. So, we cannot fight in worldly, traditional ways. There is purpose and power in our stand. Looking at Ephesians 6, we stand against the enemy's schemes; we stand without backing down; we stand against giving up. What we are standing for is so much greater! We stand for truth; we stand for hope; we stand for God's Kingdom to come and His will to be done. This stand we are taking for our own lives and the souls of our loved ones requires us to be vigilant and persistent in the spirit realm! We are warriors of a different type! Instead of "aggressively fighting" the enemy, we "aggressively stand" using the weapons of our warfare that can only be found in knowing, trusting, and believing in the Omniscient, All-powerful, Ever-present King of kings!

As we endeavor to know our awesome God deeper by spending time with Him daily, we grow to understand His heart more and more. Because of this ever-growing understanding of who He is, we can become more confident in the wielding and wearing of our spiritual armor that is mighty to tear down the strongholds of the enemy (II Corinthians 10:3-5)!

Through Him, we are righteously-upright, always-interceding, faith-filled, truth-centered, spirit-led, firmly-standing warriors! Wow! That's what the Armor of God enables us to be! Remember the Battle of Jericho in Joshua 6? The Israelites did not win that battle in a traditional way! They stood, they marched, they obeyed, and then they declared war with the pent-up energy of 7 days of silence! They did not touch Jericho's walls; yet, as they stood firm, they watched the walls tumble at their feet! Picture yourself as a confident warrior, standing at the wall of looming defeat in your life or the life of your loved one. Listen to the Lord's instruction, obey, believe, and be prepared to celebrate when your firm and confident stand results in the enemy's defeat! As you stand, even if you feel wobbly at first, know that YOU.WILL.SEE.GOD.MOVE on your behalf!

What Shall I Wear Today... and Every Day?

Don't skimp on your daily wear! Paul twice reiterates the need to put on the WHOLE armor of God! Each piece has its part and place in the believer's stand! Here is a "snapshot" of each piece in your must-have wardrobe:

Stand your ground, buckling on the Belt of Truth

The Roman soldier's belt secured his armor in place. Without this vital piece, his breastplate would swing free, his shield would have no support, and his sword and lance would clatter to the ground. Our security as believers is in the Truth! The foundation of what we stand for and believe must be rooted in the Truth of God's Word and His magnificent love for each of us who are created in His image. This first piece of armor is crucial! Righteousness, salvation, peace, and faith must be secured in Truth... without His Truth, the rest of the armor becomes ineffective.

Put on the Breastplate of Righteousness

The breastplate protects the heart and the life-giving blood that flows through the soldier's body. The Breastplate of Righteousness protects us! Our hearts should be bent on seeking His Kingdom and His righteousness first and foremost. It is our covering, our guide, and the desire that trumps all else. This laser focus helps eliminate distractors designed to weaken our stand and strengthens the protection of the prayer warrior's heart.

Pastor Eric Lehmann teaches about the two aspects of righteousness. He emphasizes that all believers stand in *positional*, or perfect, righteousness, gained through the blood of Jesus (I John 1:7). This is God's gift to us as described in Ephesians 2:8. The second aspect of righteousness is the *practical* aspect. This is the learning process and the walking out of the Lord's will and His ways (Romans 6:16, I Timothy 6:11). This aspect of righteousness is what we "put on" to set ourselves up for success. In Ephesians

4:22-24, Paul reminds us to "put off" the sinful nature and "put on" our new self. Therefore, the breastplate of righteousness declares our position of righteousness by the blood of Jesus as well as protects the heart pursuing a lifestyle of righteousness.

Put on the Shoes of the Good News of peace

The sandals of a Roman soldier were far from ordinary. The soldier's feet were firmly secured in thick-soled, heavily-studded battle shoes. Instead of worrying about slipping or slicing their feet, they could confidently stand, march, and battle. What enables believers to be sure-footed? According to Paul, it is the peace of knowing we've been reconciled to God. Romans 5:1 reminds us that we have peace with God through Jesus. When the Good News that we are at peace with the God of the Universe sinks deep into our spirits, we can stand firmly grounded and focused on His will and ways.

Above all, take up the Shield of Faith that puts out ALL the flaming arrows of the evil one:

The large, protective shield of a Roman soldier was designed to be part of a wall of protection that the front line provided in battle. The coating on these shields was specifically chosen to extinguish the flaming arrows causing them to fall harmlessly to the ground. Praying, believing, standing believers are on the front line in the spiritual battle. But we are not left unprotected! Faith in our Father God and His promises enables us to not just knock down, but to utterly extinguish the lies of the enemy! This shield of faith is also a doubt deflector. The promises of God may seem out of reach, but believe that the dreams you have not yet seen can still come to pass!

Put on the Helmet of Salvation

When headed into hand-to-hand combat, the Roman soldier was equipped with a heavy, metal helmet which could literally provide salvation when a broad sword landed a blow. When the helmet of salvation is put on, it's not getting "saved" all over again. Rather it's firmly putting on the assurance of our salvation through the blood of Jesus. As we stand firm in this spiritual battle, the enemy will attempt to disable us with doubts and condemnation. God's forgiveness is so vast that He casts our sins into the depths of the oceans! But the enemy of our souls has a great memory! As he rains down accusations, misleading thoughts, and doubt-inducing tirades, the Helmet of Salvation protects our thinking processes and allows our minds to focus on the freedom found in Jesus' redeeming work and our submission to Him as Lord and Savior!

Take the Sword of the Spirit, which is the Word of God

To this point, the armor that Paul describes has been primarily defensive. But the sword fulfills a dual role. The sword is designed to offensively take ground in a battle, bringing destruction to the enemy, all the while deflecting advances. Jesus was a prime example of this tactic. After 40 days of fasting in the wilderness, the enemy was allowed the opportunity to tempt Jesus. For each thrust of Satan's attack, Jesus parried with the truth of God's Word. At other times, He also quoted or read Scripture as He declared the

Kingdom of God had come. Reading aloud, Declaring, and Praying the Word of God are effective ways to stand strong as well as gain spiritual ground. In doing so, we are building a Kingdom vocabulary of confidence and victory. It's the Word of God that enables us to defeat doubt, topple temptation, and halt our hopelessness (Hebrews 4:12).

Pray on all occasions with all kinds of prayers and requests

In reading the text, this command seems tacked on as an afterthought. But, oh how vital our prayers are in this spiritual battle! The one piece of Roman armor that Paul doesn't mention is the javelin. In referencing this scripture, Lehmann proposes that the javelin represents the prayers of the stander's heart. The javelin was a weapon that the soldiers would thrust ahead of them to take out enemy soldiers in advance, further ensuring their success. Likewise, our prayers are sent forth to accomplish a work in the spiritual realm further ensuring an accomplished work in the physical realm. James 5:16 encourages us that the prayers of a righteous (right-standing) person are powerful and effective. Picture yourself as that warrior, actively standing, thrusting the javelin of prayer effectively and with power! Keep sending forth those prayers in the Spirit, on all occasions, about all that is in your heart. God's strategies are without fail!

Once we are "dressed" in the Lord and in the power of His might, we stand alert, ready for instructions, persistently praying. Though seemingly a paradox, it's this active stand that results in advances in the spiritual realms!

Can You... Will You Stand Firm?

Consider this: Could it be that <u>your</u> stand of confidence and <u>your</u> prayers of faith will be the ones to pave the way for the prodigal to find their way back home to the Father? What an exciting possibility and opportunity!

Knowing that your precious loved one is living away from the Father's love is heartbreaking! You may be longing to have the relationship with them restored; yet, it is more vital that their relationship with the Father is restored! We cannot judge their salvation or the state of their soul... it's not our place. But we know that the Word is clear about the destruction that the prodigal's choices can and will cause. But God!!! He cares deeply for these missing ones and longs to have them home. He hears our prayers as we cooperate with His plans and purposes.

With this thought in mind, I'd like to share a prayer for the prodigal in your life. Whether it's a father, mother, child, friend, sibling, or spouse, it should be our heart's cry that they would come home to the Father's heart. I'm a firm believer that declaring the Word out loud causes ripples in the spirit realm, where many things become manifest before we see them in the physical realm. So, I encourage you to read this prayer out loud, inserting your loved one's name. Declare it often, believing that God's Word will not return void, but will accomplish what He desires!

A Prayer for the Prodigal

Dear Lord, I lift up _____ to You today! Your Word says that since I'm made in Your image, I can call things forth as though they are (Romans 4:17, II Cor. 4:13), so I declare these things over _____!

Father, I declare You love him/her deeply and passionately. You have a plan to prosper his/her life with a hope and a future. So, I believe that _____ would call upon You and You would bring him/her back from his/her captivity (Jeremiah 29:11-14).

I ask that You'd render the enemy impotent in _____'s life. I pray that You would remove the enemy's blinders so that truth and revelation will pierce his/her heart and spirit. I bind up confusion and lies in Jesus' name and loose Truth to _____ by your Holy Spirit. Father, I ask that You'd grant repentance to _____ that he/she would know the Truth, come to his/her senses, and escape the snare of the devil (II Tim. 2:25b-26, Luke 15:17). Lord, please bring him/her to a place of godly sorrow that leads to this true repentance (II Cor. 7:10).

You said that _____ would have a willing heart of flesh and You would put Your Spirit in him/her that he/she would want to walk in all Your ways for the rest of his/her life. (Ezekiel 36:25-27) Lord, I believe that _____ will love you totally and completely as his/her First Love and there will be no luke-warmness in him/her. Father, I declare that _____'s spirit hungers and thirsts for righteousness (Matt. 5:6). He/she will trust in You always and delight him/herself in You so that he/she can receive the desires of his/her heart (Psalm 37:3-4). I thank You that his/her heart is healed by You. I thank You that Your purposes for _____ will prevail (Prov. 19:21).

I declare that _____ will walk in repentance, compassion, integrity, purity, and truth. He/she will walk in his/her destiny as a mighty man/woman of God. I am thankful that _____ will hear Your voice and choose to daily walk in Your truth. Greater are You in _____ than he that is in the world. I know Your perfect love never fails and that You desire that _____ would not perish (II Peter 3:9). I believe these things and call them done in the mighty name of Jesus! Thank You, Lord!

On a Side Note

It's quite possible that you have no desire for the prodigal to be part of your life again, especially in the same way that they were in the past. The damage may be too great. No one can fault you for such caution or concern. God gives us wisdom to set boundaries when necessary.

However, don't miss the blessing that can be had in knowing that your prayers on the prodigal's behalf rise as sweet incense to the Father! Even if you are never aware of the impact of those prayers on earth, the seed you are sowing will reap eternal benefits. Of all the choices in your life that you may regret, you will never regret being a part of the redemptive process! So, lift up prayers for the prodigals in your life! Whether they are repentant or not, whether they feel they are in need or not, whether they are near or far away… God longs for their return to Him and you have an opportunity to cooperate with the heart of the Father on their behalf!

My prayer for you

Dear Loving Father, Thank You for Your love and forgiveness! Thank You for restoring this reader each and every time they've sought Your face. I pray that You would strengthen their resolve to be an instrument of restoration and redemption. May your ear be turned to their prayers. Where there is despair, I speak hope! Where there is discouragement, I speak life! Thank You, Lord, that You can make a way where there seems to be no way! Our eyes are on You! In Jesus' Name, Amen!

Activation and Application

Read:

- James 5:13-20
- II Corinthians 7:9-12

Consider:

- Am I purposeful about filling my mind with Truth from God's Word each day?
- Do I understand what the will of God is for me as His child?
- What are two practical ways I can daily "transform" my mind to be in sync with the Holy Spirit? (Hebrews 12:1-2)

Declaration

Father, I thank You that You love me despite my mistakes. I ask that You would pierce my heart with godly sorrow that leads to repentance when I make choices that don't align with Your ways. Help me to walk according to Your Word all the days of my life. I trust that Your ways are best and that Your Word is true! I love You, Lord!

6

The Humble Heart: Accepting Responsibility

"Your character should always be stronger than your circumstances."[7]
-Dave Willis

Have you ever seen a tree so ripe with fruit that its branches are sagging? Look closer... the fruit is labeled: Love, joy, peace, patience, kindness, goodness, faithfulness, gentleness, and self-control... Wouldn't it be great if that tree was reflective of you and me? I wish I could say that these are the characteristics I exude when others spill my coffee, rain on my parade, and trample my hurting heart. But I know the truth. Instead of demonstrating sweet fruits, I'm afraid I've responded by throwing rotten tomatoes and raw eggs! Like you, I've got a laundry list of excuses for my choices, but that doesn't make them wise... or harmless.

This may be a bitter pill to swallow, but rarely ever can a prodigal take ALL the responsibility for a failing relationship. The adage: "It takes two to tango" proves to be true more often than not. No matter if your prodigal is a cheating spouse, a drug-addicted parent, or a blame-projecting sibling, you and I have made mistakes that did not help the prodigal's struggle. In our humanity, we too often react out of hurt, anger, fear, or frustration. Some of these errors may be long in the past and some may be much more recent. For this reason, offering an apology is not only quite appropriate but also necessary.

Please know two important things:

1. Humbling yourself and offering a sincere apology opens doors of communication. The recipient of your apology may or may not receive your comments. They may respond in anger, sarcasm, or shock. But regardless, you've offered peace in spite of pain. By taking ownership of your choices and mistakes, you become more approachable to your beloved prodigal.

2. Humbling yourself in authentic repentance demonstrates the heart of the Father. What is the heart of the Father? Simply put: Love! It's choosing to love another regardless of their actions. It's understanding and accepting that our actions may have been more detrimental to the relationship than we realize and valuing that relationship enough to facilitate healing.

On a side note: Apologizing to someone does not necessarily mean inviting them back into your circle of security. This is particularly true if there has been physical, sexual, emotional, or mental abuse. When you humble yourself, you are admitting to your own errors in judgement and responses born out of pain. You are not inviting the other person to enter relationship in the same way you may have in the past. We will explore this idea more in a later chapter.

Anointed Insight

Apologies are difficult. They often require a fair amount of mental gymnastics to sort through our own feelings and understandings. This is one of the many areas that I believe Divine counsel is helpful. Ask the Lord to remind you of things you have said or done that may have been considered hurtful or judgmental in the eyes of the prodigal. Remember that it's often not about how or why you made those choices, but rather it's about how the other person perceived your actions and words. Those are the aspects that you'll need the Lord to reveal to you.

Another thought to consider is how your apology should be delivered. This is highly dependent upon your current relationship, or lack of relationship, with the prodigal you are interceding for in prayer. Possibilities include electronic (email or private message) written letter, phone call, or in person. Will your loved one be more receptive of one over the other? When should you offer your apology? Those are questions best brought before the Lord for careful consideration and direction. (Cautionary note: Avoid texts as they are notoriously misunderstood due to their brevity.)

I've included here an apology that came out of my heart. It can be easily adapted and personalized with more specification where needed. Think of it as a place to start!

An Apology to the Prodigal

I'm sorry! I've not treated you with the love of the Father. Honestly, I'm struggling with my own confusion, pain, and doubts. I truly want to represent God's love to you but I'm having a hard time figuring out the best way to do that. I want to tell you that "It's all good," but I'd be lying. I want to tell you, "I understand," but I don't. I want to say that "Everything can be like it was before," but that's unrealistic. So, I really don't know what to say.

My heart hurts. Is yours hurting too? I regret that I may have caused you some of that pain. Please forgive me. Forgive my impatience, judgmental attitude, unkind words, and lack of understanding. I know my reactions have not been helpful. I've made mistakes.

I realize now that the only person I can work on… the only person I can change… is me. So, that's my goal. I want to be more like Jesus. I need His grace like never before! I need to understand His love for each of us so that I can show that love to those around me. I long to be an encouragement to our hurting world. I want you to know that I love you and I want to show you that love somehow, someday. Please be patient with me as I walk out this journey… It's a learning process and I've got a long way to go.

My prayer for you

Dear Lord, This journey of seeing clearly our own actions and the pain they may have caused, can be a difficult and painful one. I pray that You would gently speak to this reader! Direct their mind's eye to see and remember choices that brought pain to the prodigal so that he/she can make amends to the best of his/her ability. Please bring Your peace as he/she chooses to humble his/herself and become a peacemaker. Thank You, Father!

Activation and Application

Read:

- Proverbs 18:21
- Galatians 5:22-23
- Colossians 3:12-17

Consider:

- Am I finding comfort in comparing myself to others? To whom or what should my standard of behavior be aligned?
- Based on the above Scriptures, what are some aspects of my character that need to grow in the Lord?

Declaration:

Lord, Your Word says that You will not despise a contrite or teachable heart (Psalm 51). I come to You willing to be humbled and taught. I pray that You will give me Your wisdom and insight. Pave the way for me to be a peacemaker. Make _____'s heart receptive to the healing words that I bring. Thank You, Father, for Your hand in this situation.

7

The Hungry Heart: Pursuing Relationship

"God is more concerned with our process than our problems."
- Joy Morey

He was a little ticked off, the big brother… after all, dad's having a party for the vagrant scoundrel who ran off and spent nearly half of dad's money! When was the last time dad had given him a party?

The perpetual son… he hadn't left, hadn't partied, and hadn't wasted his inheritance. His only crime was being a bit jealous, right? As I meditated on this parable of the forgiving father, the repentant son, and the dutiful brother, the Lord challenged my heart. You see, there are several things the perpetual brother hadn't done that kept him in good standing with the father. But there are other things that he also hadn't done that left him out in the cold when his runaway brother returned. In fact, the father didn't even call for the brother to come to the prodigal's celebration. I had to ask myself, "Why not?"

The perpetual son was dutiful, hardworking, and honorable, right? So, why wasn't he invited? I believe this is why: Even though this son remained at home, he hadn't cultivated his relationship with his father. How do I know this? Because, the dutiful son did not carry the father's heart for his brother. Instead, he carried a heart of righteous indignation, anger, and hurt. Were his feelings wrong? Not initially. However, allowing those feelings to fester in his heart created a judgmental attitude towards his brother. This attitude stole the opportunity to rejoice when his brother returned. He missed out on the blessing of seeing his father's eyes fill with joyful tears.

We've seen that this parable is indicative of the incredible love the Heavenly Father has for us. When we think about it or read it, we tend to place ourselves in either the prodigal child or perpetual child category. I don't want to be in either! I want to be the purposeful child! It's not enough for you and I to be simply dutiful… saved and working for His Kingdom. I want to cultivate a vibrant, powerful, loving relationship with my Father!

"Sure, I'll go out to the field and work. But can we sit and have coffee together first, Dad? Can I pray with You about our prodigal (brother, sister, child, parent, or spouse)? Can I hear Your heart for them? Will You please help my heart to heal?"

This may be a news flash for you: God is not only interested in your prodigal's heart… He is interested in working in your heart too! We haven't arrived just because we are not running from Him. It's not enough to "not run" from God, we need to purposefully pursue Him and His ways! Stagnant, or still, waters become polluted and lifeless cesspools. You and I need to allow His living waters to flow in and out of us daily.

Even though things may be difficult, don't miss the blessing of this season in your life. There's beauty found in these ashes… that beauty is in drawing closer to the Lord than you've ever been before! It is in coming to know Him as the Lover of your soul and the Keeper of your heart. The work He desires to do in you may be uncomfortable, and even painful, but submitting to His skillful Hand will benefit you and your loved ones more than you can imagine!

I want to remain so close to my Father that when a missing one comes home, He turns to me with joy in His eyes and gives me a high five! "Yes, My Child, your lost brother/sister has come Home! Let's celebrate!"

My prayer for you

Daddy, You are so amazing! Your loving-kindness continues to draw us in every stage of life. I ask that this precious reader would feel Your presence even now guiding them, ministering to them, and strengthening them! I pray that there would be no waste in this season, but that each situation would drive them closer to You! Let their heart hunger and thirst for all that You are and have for them. In Jesus' precious name, I ask these things!

Activation and Application

Read:

- John 15:1-17
- Ephesians 3:14-21

Consider:

- How does the Lord see me… as a prodigal child, a perpetual child or a purposeful child?
- What can I do today to purposely pursue a deeper relationship with the Father?
- What are the areas of my heart or life that the Lord has been whispering to me about but I've been ignoring?

Declaration:

My Precious Father, Heal my heart, I pray. Help me to walk in forgiveness towards those that have hurt me. Give me Your heart and vision for them. It's Your desire that none should perish without You, so I pray that each prodigal in my life would return to Your loving arms. Help me to know You more each day and give me a revelation of the deep love You have for me! I love You, Dad! Thanks for loving me!

8

The Healing Heart: The Productive Process

"There comes a time in your life when you need to make what Jesus did for you greater than what someone did to you."[8]
- Christine Caine

Imagine with me… you are meandering along a dirt pathway through barren woods. The trees are bare and a cold wind rattles the empty branches. The dreary lifelessness tugs at your lonely, aching soul. You're tempted to curl up in a ball and hide under the debris on the ground. Suddenly, you look ahead… up there, in the distance, you sense warmth; you see light, life, color!

But it's a long way off… what would you do?

If you're tempted to plop down right where you are and wallow in a bit of self-pity, you would not be the first! The effort of pressing on to healing and living life again may seem like too much when you have so little energy in your reserves. But healing does not just "come" to us. It's something we must move toward and even pursue. Light, life, and color are ahead but the only way to reach it is to press on.

This chapter is not a comprehensive approach to healing and forgiveness. But there are nuggets of truth here that will set you well on the path of healing. You may need to seek a trustworthy counselor to work through your feelings and to come to grips with your new normal. Remember that a journey is a process, a pathway that is leading us somewhere. You may stop and rest for a bit in the middle, but then get up and keep moving!

The Path to Healing

The path to healing starts with a step forward! Be it big, small, stumbling, or firm… acknowledging your need to forgive and heal starts you down this road (Chapter 3 discusses this in more depth). There might be some bumps and setbacks, but the journey in itself can be a time of growth and revelation.

Know this: Your healing is NOT contingent on the actions of the prodigal in your life! Understand that he or she may never work towards restoration with you. However, do not allow that possibility to hinder your healing process.

While healing can be facilitated and even spurred along by a repentant prodigal, we cannot rely on the actions of others to move forward in our own journey. Taking ownership of your role in the process will be what propels you down this path.

Lean into the Pain

During my journey to healing, I gained a wise piece of advice from a speaker at a conference. She said, "Don't try to avoid the pain… instead, lean into it." This can be applied to so many areas of life! We spend a fair amount of time trying to avoid things we consider distasteful or painful.

So, what is to be gained from "leaning into" or accepting the pain?

- **Time:** Leaning into your pain will move you down the path of healing in a timelier manner. We tend to dilly-dally with distractions to avoid doing the actions we truly cannot avoid if we want to know real healing in our lives. In a way, it's like moving your dentist appointment up so that you can take care of a painful tooth sooner. Delay just means a longer process. Denial is a waste of time and energy. You are hurting! Accept it. Own it. Keep moving forward!

- **Patience:** When we try to avoid pain, it doesn't go away. What it does do is ooze out in other areas and spill onto those who don't deserve it. Acknowledging and even embracing pain allows us to release it in bits and pieces appropriately. Leaning into the pain enables you to avoid venting your anger or hurt on the innocent bystander. We learn that acknowledging the pain allows us to cope with it in manageable amounts. It is a preferable alternative to shoving the pain down until the intense pressure builds up to a volcanic magnitude and erupts on our precious loved ones and friends.

- **Health:** Releasing tension caused by emotional hurt should be done in healthy ways such as crying, singing, exercising, talking, dancing, or writing. When we try to avoid pain instead of embracing it, unhealthy choices such as excessive drinking, drugs, smoking, gambling, and overeating may become life-destroying habits. Addictive habits simply numb the pain for a short time just to have it come back with renewed impact.

- **Reality:** Denying pain may seem to be something the hopeful idealist should do. Alternatively, wallowing in pain seems to be the perpetual pessimist's approach. But this optimist knows that embracing pain is a middle of the road approach… it's just being real! When we hurt, it's okay to admit that sometimes life hurts. Denying it is foolish, as is wailing it from the heavens. Be real without being maudlin. There's something freeing about being honest with yourself and those you trust.

- **Authentic relationship:** When you lean into the pain, you are being authentic. Someone else in your life could use a dose of that authentic you. Tap into a tried-and-true friend who will walk this journey with you. Let them hold you when you cry, be a sounding board for your angry moments, and a light of encouragement when you feel lost in the darkness. You'll find that there's a time when they will need you to do the same. When you come through to the other side, you'll have a cohort in the victory celebration!

Grief: It's about to get real!

Often, we think of the grieving process as only happening after someone dies. However, the grief process happens as a result of a myriad of "deaths" during our lifetime. Consider these "deaths:"

- The loss of a home
- Relocating to a new city, state, or country
- The end of a career
- A life-changing illness
- Behavioral Diagnosis
- Failure to conceive
- A dream never realized
- A home or person being violated
- Bankruptcy of a business

These are all traumatic events that require a grieving process. When you experience pain or loss in a precious relationship, you too, must grieve. The process of grieving is generally considered to include five stages:

1. Denial
2. Anger
3. Bargaining
4. Depression
5. Acceptance

These stages can occur in quick succession or one stage may be significantly longer than another and the pattern may repeat more than once. Grief is its own unique "animal" and different for each person. It shows up when it wants and leaves you feeling like a wrung-out rag. But like the waves on the shoreline, just as it comes, it will go back out again. Eventually the waves of grief will come less often and with less intensity.

Self-awareness is vital to any healing process. Research the stages of grief. Invite your trusted friend to discuss the symptoms with you as well as help you ascertain where in the process you may be and if you need to pursue professional support. Being aware of the process and identifying what stage you are in currently, will enable you to understand more of your journey. A bonus benefit is that this deeper understanding of your process will help cultivate healthy interactions with your loved ones.

Refreshment: Be sure to grab some!

If you're not careful your entire wealth of energy will be absorbed by dwelling on your painful circumstances… replaying scenes in your mind, evaluating conversations, plotting future actions, and imagining a myriad of scenarios. You must call a halt to the mental gymnastics from time to time. Choose to relax and spend a bit of time in a place of temporary denial of your situation… in other words, find refreshment! I know you're overwhelmed; I know you don't have a lot of time to just relax; I know life may be very painful right now. However, to endure for the long haul, you must determine to give your mind and heart a reprieve.

I've never run an actual marathon, nor do I intend to! But I've run an emotional marathon and if you are on the path to healing, you are running one too. In a marathon, there are water stations strategically placed to refresh the runner without slowing them down. You need to discover what activities will enable you to find refreshment without slowing down your journey. During your healing marathon, these refreshment stations will energize your soul and help boost your lagging spirits.

Personally, I found music to be a wonderful source of refreshment! Songs that were encouraging, uplifting, and truth-filled gave me moments of weeping, comfort, and ultimately peace. Walking outdoors was also healing and restful for me. You may find that reading allows your soul to rest. Refreshment may come from a bike ride, watching a sporting event, going for a hike, or even rearranging furniture. Something as simple as cleaning out a junk drawer or as complex as landscaping a yard might be just what you need as a boost of refreshment in this journey. Experiment, explore, engage… don't bypass those opportunities for refreshment. They offer you the sustaining power to not just survive, but thrive in your healing journey.

The Audience

Don't look now, but you're being watched. Rarely does the runner care or notice, but along the sides of the route, are the watchers. As you travel the pathway of healing, you have an audience. Some might be cheering you on while others are hissing. Most need to be ignored.

Except for… those precious ones in your realm of influence. No matter the depth or breadth of your pain, if you have people in your life dependent on your example and influence, then your journey impacts them as well as yourself. Be cognizant of that influence and carry it close to your heart. Whether they are a child or an adult, they are most likely seeking healing too. As you choose to forgive, to lean into the pain, to grieve, and to pursue healing; they are watching, learning, absorbing. They need you… you need them. Stay the course! Your victory will be theirs as well!

My prayer for you

Dear Lord, You created this precious friend in Your image! You know the depth of their hurt and desperate need for healing. I pray, Father, that as they pursue the path of healing, You will guide them, sustain them, and fill their hearts with the light of Your life! I pray that You will help them navigate the rocky areas with grace and wisdom. Give them insight and direction. Bring people into their lives that will offer Your encouragement and truth. Heal their hearts and the hearts of those they love, I pray. Thank You, Awesome Father! In Jesus' Name, Amen.

Activation and Application

Read:

- Isaiah 58:6-9
- Psalm 23
- I Peter 5:6-10

Consider:

- Would I benefit from learning more about the grieving process?
- Who are two tried and true people that will encourage me in my journey of healing?
- What are 2-3 ways that I am confident will help me find refreshment in my healing marathon?

Declaration:

Dear Heavenly Father, Thank You for Your incredible love and Your healing power! I ask You to wrap my wounded heart in Your healing hands. Give me wisdom and insight into this journey. Help me to hear Your direction, to listen, and to obey. I trust You, Lord! You are faithful even when I fail. I thank You, today, for my healing! I believe it will come and I will walk in faith knowing I will be made whole again. Thank You, Jesus!

9

The Heart with Vision: Speaking Life

"The words you speak will create the path you walk on."[9]
- Eric Lehmann

Imagine… it's a Super Bowl Halftime and the team that's behind trudges into the locker room. The head coach stands before the dispirited team determining how to inspire and motivate. He can ream his team out for their unproductive choices, highlighting all the errors that led up to their 14-point deficit. Or… he can encourage them that the second half is a fresh slate to make better choices, reminding them of their past success and his confidence in their future victory. If you're a player sitting on the bench, feeling tired and worn down, which speech do you need to hear?

In the beginning of time, God created the world with His very words. He spoke to seedlings and they budded!

He called forth animals and they appeared! He exhaled life and Adam breathed! This was the most exciting part, found in Genesis 1:26-27, when God said, "Let Us make man in Our image, according to Our likeness." He truly is our Daddy! He created us to bear the image of His character! When this truth settles into our spirits, a hunger will stir to investigate who God truly is and how we can be His reflection to the world around us.

God demonstrated to us that He calls things that do not exist as though they did (Romans 4:17, Hebrews 11:3). Job 22:27-28 reminds us that we can declare a thing and it will be established (NKJV). After God created man, He gave us dominion, or authority, over all the earth. Being able to create with our words is a powerful gift; one that can be used for good or evil, life or death. Tucked away in Proverbs is this truth: "The tongue has the power of life and death" (Proverbs 18:21a).

This popular adage has been tossed around over the past fifty years or so: "The best way to predict the future is to create it." The basis of this quote originates with Jesus when He states, "Let it be done just as you believed it would" (Matthew 8:13). Jesus knew that we conceive our future in our thoughts before it ever begins to transpire. Pair that idea with this thought: the mouth speaks what is in the heart (Luke 6:45, Matthew 12:34). What you believe in your heart and mind is what comes out of your mouth. You create your future when your thoughts form into words! Stop and think… what kind of future is your mind seeing? What kind of future is your mouth declaring? What are you speaking over your relationships? What are you declaring about your prodigal? What are you predicting about your health? What are you expecting for your finances? If you've been a "Negative Nelly" or "Downer Dan," it's time to hit the brakes on the death talk! It's time to SPEAK LIFE!

Establish a Plan!

Speaking life involves declaring the truth of God's Word over our lives and situations. It includes making positive declarations even when our eyes see evidence to the contrary. Remember that faith is a conviction of things we haven't yet seen. That's what makes faith so challenging! When we speak life to a situation, we are declaring in faith, that good things are coming, even though it looks like an impossibility.

Remember that struggling Super Bowl team? To find success in the 2nd half of the game, the team will need encouragement and a plan! To move forward in your life, relationships, finances, and career, you need words of encouragement and a plan! It's time to move forward in confidence!

Encouragement is like a two-sided coin. On the one hand, there are times when we need to be like King David and simply encourage ourselves in the Lord (Psalm 18). Instead of picking up a cellphone, we tap into the Encourager (Holy Spirit) and dive into the Scriptures, building up our spirit man with the promises of God and His faithfulness. Learning to develop our encouragement muscles is part of maturing as believers.

On the flip side is the need to build a team of encouragers around us. What a blessing it is to have a support system when we are struggling or be the support to someone else going through a difficult time! Unless you enjoy being eaten by the lion (John 10:10), avoid being a lone wolf! Be purposeful in finding other like-minded believers who will encourage and speak life to you when the pain and disappointments of life seem overwhelming. Both sides of the encouragement coin are valid and needed.

Implement the Plan!

Not having a plan is planning to fail. Setting a plan in motion enables us to develop the purposeful practice that brings success. The "Speak Life" plan has three key steps. Like any new habit, it will take some time and effort, but the good news is that you can start today! You may not see instant results, but know that when you sow good things, you will reap good things if you do not give up (Galatians 6:9)!

1. Believe: What is Your Outlook?

You might be struggling to imagine that good things are in store for you. The enemy of our souls would like nothing more than to keep you disheartened and hopeless.

So, how can we be confident that good things are coming? Romans chapter 8 is a powerful statement about how God feels about us… He loves you! He loves me! Our hope is in God and His faithfulness! When we love Him and are submitting our lives to His purpose and plan, we can trust that every situation, good or bad, will work out for our good. He is trustworthy and faithful, even when we have failed (II Timothy 2:13)! This is the first step of the

"Speak Life" plan: Realize that God not only loves you, He likes you and has great plans for you! Dig deep into the wells of His love and allow the Holy Spirit to minister to those doubting places. Good things are in store for you… that's an outlook worth finding!

Recognizing and embracing God's intense and unconditional love is the launching pad, but it's only the start. In an effort to launch the "Speak Life" Plan, a logical place to start would be: "Just say good things." Seems like it should be rather easy, right? On upbeat days, it can be. You know those days… things are going well, the kids are listening, the bills are paid, and no one gets in your way on the commute to work! Positive is easy on those sunshine-and-rainbow days!

But life has its fair share of thunderstorm-and-raincloud days. These days can feel overwhelming when we are dealing with a relational trauma. When our "cups" are full of stress, it only takes a slight nudge for the frustration to spill over, too often flowing through our words. How easily we slip back into doubt and discouragement and we let it run like lava from our mouths. It's time for step two, time to reprogram our thinking patterns!

2. Think: What are your Thought Habits?

Our perspective, or outlook, is subjective to and at the mercy of our thoughts, experiences, hurts, even motivations.

Any coach will tell you that skills are perfected through consistent, persistent, and purposeful practice. Step two of the "Speak Life" plan involves changing thought patterns. You may have practiced wrong thinking for a long time, so be patient with yourself and realize that right thinking will take lots of practice too. Filling our minds with truth based on God's Word is vital. His Word is water to our thirsty souls! As we meditate on the truths found in God's Word, allowing the Spirit to download those truths past our mind into our spirits, life begins to flood our thinking and change our perspective. Thus, begins the reprogramming of our thought patterns from death to life!

God's Word is full of powerful revelation that impacts our day to day lives. Meditating, absorbing, and embracing those truths can happen in different ways. Here are a few ideas to try:

- Listen to an auditory presentation of God's Word
- Memorize Scripture
- Post Scriptures in highly visible areas of your home
- Write verses in a journal
- Listen to and/or sing Scripture based songs
- Use creative expression such as drawing or painting a verse
- Pray Scriptures back to the Lord
- Underline or circle Scriptures in your Bible and write notes in the margins

Don't underestimate the value of these simple exercises. God's Word is a source of life in itself!

3. Speak: What are Your Words Creating?

The "Speak Life" plan step three involves purposefully and consistently declaring the truths that are becoming established as thought patterns. As your thinking changes and Godly truths take root in your mind, your mouth will begin to speak life into your family, your job situation, your finances, your friendships, and your destiny! Develop a vocabulary of success that will bring hope, faith, and life to the forefront of your thinking, ultimately altering your perspective and experience of day to day events and circumstances.

Consistently, persistently, and purposefully speaking positive words will become a habit and life will flow out of your spirit, bringing blessing on yourself and those in your realm of influence! What an exciting opportunity and privilege! A wholesome, kind, wise, and gentle tongue is a tree of life and promotes health (Proverbs 12:18b, 15:4)!

The Source of Change

You've heard the adage: Inside every rain cloud is a silver lining. Speaking life means choosing to focus on that silver lining despite the threatening raincloud. This is a shift in mindset from doubt and fear to faith and confidence. Attempting this shift on our own will produce frustrating and short-lived results. **It is the work of the Holy Spirit in you that will bring about this critical change.** With this thought in mind, let me encourage you to daily pursue a deeper relationship with Jesus! He longs to know you and be known by you. Hebrews 11:6 tells us that the Lord is a Rewarder of those who earnestly seek Him! In knowing Him, truly knowing Jesus and His ways, everything else falls into place!

My prayer for you

Dear Father, Thank You for Your amazing, all-encompassing, deep love for us! You call us sons and daughters and Your love is unconditional! Give this precious reader a revelation of Your love today and a confidence that You will cause every situation in their life to work together for good as they submit their lives to You. Make their ears open to the ministering of Your Holy Spirit as He speaks truth into their spirits. Thank You, Daddy, that Your ways are perfect and You are trustworthy!

Activation and Application

Read:

- Proverbs 16:3, 18:21
- II Timothy 3:16-17

Consider:

- What kind of declarations am I making over my life? Positive or negative?
- What reminders can I put into place to remind myself of the need to purposefully "Speak Life?"
- Write down some words or statements that you want to add to your vocabulary of success. They may be as simple as, "Thank You, God, that You are in control," or more situation focused such as, "Thank You for providing the finances for the tires I need."

Declaration:

Dear Father, Thank You for the deep love that I've read about in Your Word. Thank You that You do have good things in store for me! Help me commit myself to knowing You deeper and to learning and dwelling on Your truths. Enable me to speak life over my family, my finances, my relationships, and my job situation. I declare that Life will flow from my tongue according to Your Word and Your work in me! I want to know You more and more! Thank You, Lord! In Jesus' Name, Amen!

10

The Heart of Restoration: New but Purposeful Normal

"Love doesn't erase the past but it makes the future different."[10]
- Gary Chapman

Have you ever endured an earthquake? One moment the world is calm and orderly, and a split-second later, disorder and chaos reign as furniture topples and screams rent the air. Hours, days, and even weeks later, tremors may still be felt, sometimes real, sometimes imagined. Earthquake survivors experience a new normal… one that includes wariness. Permanence is an illusion; stability is temperamental; life can change in a blink of an eye. The once confident stride proceeds a little more carefully amid a world of potential tremors.

The longer we are alive, the more of this reality we understand. Life's traumas demand that we adapt and learn to live in a new normal. We rarely get to choose WHAT the new normal is, but we can choose HOW we will live it. Purposeful living is determining not to simply exist, but to live and thrive regardless of our circumstances. It involves engaging in healthy relationships and promoting the restoration of hurting ones.

Sounds simple, right? But when you're down for the count, gasping for breath from a direct hit, survival is all you're focused on. It's okay! No one expects you to jump up, give a high-five to your circumstances, and dive back into the game. You need some time to sit still, rest, recoup, catch your breath. How much time? Each person and circumstance is different. Just don't stay down forever!

Solomon, the wise poet, reminds us that there's a season for everything. There's a time to weep and a time to laugh, a time to mourn and a time to dance, a time to tear and a time to mend (Ecclesiastes 3). Your season of rest and healing is a time for you to engage with the Lord and see His hand at work in your heart and circumstances. The temptation may be to stay in a cocoon of wariness, avoiding a world of potential pain tremors. But this is not thriving. Through God's grace and wisdom, you can have your confident stride restored! You can boldly move forward in God's plans and purposes for your life.

Realize that it's quite possible that those purposes will include interactions with the prodigal in your life. We cannot underestimate the power of the enemy's deception. Some prodigals will convince themselves that they are exactly where God wants them to be. Some prodigals will recognize their errors but have made decisions that they cannot or will not abandon. No matter where your prodigal is or what their choices are, it's your responsibility to move forward in your life and healing with a purposeful heart. The heart of restoration involves having positive and healthy interactions with a prodigal whether they are repentant or not.

What About Love?

Making choices is not optional and nearly every choice we make affects those around us. Sometimes those choices hurt the loved ones in our lives, even if that was never our intent. In the same way, the prodigal's choices affect us. Most likely, the motivator was not to cause us pain, but rather to live life on their own terms. Yet, their choices are still heartbreaking. Naturally, when we experience pain, our response is to pull back.

This reflex reaction includes the tendency to withdraw our love. In our minds, love equates approval. Think about it: When our parents were proud of us, they hugged us! When we pleased a teacher or coach, they proclaimed their pride and "love." When we give a desired gift, we get a response of love and thanks. Approval is repeatedly associated with love. The last thing we want to do is allow our wandering loved one to believe that we are okay with their choices! So, we turn a cold shoulder, fold our arms across our chest, and make our disapproval clear. However, this stance of disapproval shouts, "There's no love for you anymore!" even if that is not our intent.

The approval-equals-love understanding is performance based. "I will be loved when I'm good enough." "God will love me if I pray more." "My dad will be proud of me when I accomplish my goals." This pull-yourself-up-by-the-bootstraps mentally is pervasive in the American culture. It's also a classic and effective tool of the enemy of our souls. Satan knows that if he can undermine our understanding of God's love, he can derail our faith, confidence, relationships, and ultimately, our effectiveness in the Kingdom of God.

This thinking highlights our misunderstanding of what true, authentic love is. Unconditional love simply says, "I love you, just because." There are no qualifiers, no expectations, no conditions. Wow! This is the kind of love the Heavenly Father gives us AND requires us to give others! In fact, I Corinthians 13 declares that if we do not have love, we are noise makers, who will gain nothing, no matter what we do! Does that challenge you as much as it does me?

In Luke 6, Jesus leaves us little doubt about how to treat the ones who've hurt us. He calls us to love, bless, and give! He expects us to be merciful and kind; regardless of how we have been treated! This is no easy task, even when someone acknowledges they've caused us pain.

What's more challenging is that God expects us to love the prodigal, repentant or not! We must come to understand that loving the prodigal does not condone the choices that they have made. Loving the prodigal demonstrates that they are precious in our mind because of who they are, not because of what they do or give. Determining that value… giving that unconditional love… must be a reflection of our relationship with our Heavenly Father! Otherwise, you will find it a nearly impossible task.

With a purposeful mindset and the restoration goal, we must determine to show this love. So, how do we demonstrate such love…
- Despite our pain,
- Without showing approval,
- Minus our anger,
- Disregarding attitude,
- While promoting healing,

…All without letting our trust-guard down?

Fight the Good Fight!

Some things are worth the fight! But you must use strategies that breed success. Paul says that we are battling in the spirit realm and encourages us to arm ourselves with the Armor of God (Review Chapter 5: "Taking a Stand"), stand firm, and to pray (Ephesians 6)! These strategies are all mental and spiritual exercises; but they bring forth fruit in the physical realm!

Too often, we spend energy reserves replaying previous encounters or planning future encounters in our minds. These mental exercises are fruitless. To demonstrate godly love to the prodigals in our lives, we must proactively prepare ourselves prior to encounters. By steeping our hearts and minds in prayer, we can be prepped and ready to allow His Spirit of love to flow through our actions and through our words. Prepare by choosing to think loving thoughts regarding your prodigal. Stock up on positive thoughts and promises from God's Word about your loved one. Practice speaking life to them and to the situation. This front-loading of revelatory truth enables us to avoid the lack-of-love pitfalls (rudeness, irritability, grudge-holding, and pride) and allows us to demonstrate the lots-of-love advances (patience, kindness, hope, and endurance).

This love states, "I accept you as a beloved creation of our Heavenly Father." By demonstrating this love, you are not approving of their choices. You are not celebrating their mistakes. You are not erasing their painful blows. Rather, you are choosing to reflect authentic love despite all of these things. This kind of love DOES NOT FAIL! Because it is God's love flowing through you. Be a conduit… allow His love to move from Him to you and then through you to the prodigal!

How can you manage to love like this? One thought at a time. One prayer at a time. One kind word at a time. One encounter at a time. The Lord will give you the necessary grace at the very moment it's required. The closer you walk with Him, the easier it is to tap into all that He has for you!

"I keep asking that the God of our Lord Jesus Christ, the glorious Father, may give you the Spirit of wisdom and revelation, so that you may know Him better. I pray that the eyes of your heart may be enlightened in order that you may know the hope to which He has called you, the riches of His glorious inheritance in His holy people, and His incomparably great power for us who believe" (Ephesians 1:17-19a).

May God give you the spirit of wisdom and revelation so that you may know Him better, that your heart may be enlightened so that you would know the hope to which He has called you! And that you would get a vibrant, resounding, revelation of His great power for you as a believer! Through Him, you are able to love unconditionally!

The Non-Repentant Prodigal

Your loved one may choose to stay in the "far country" for far longer than you could have thought. Deceptive dreams can hinder the prodigal's return home. False contentment, fear, disillusionment, guilt, and condemnation all act as invisible restraints that keep the prodigal far from the Father's love. Their wandering journey may keep them in this place for months, years, even decades.

What can you and I do? Never give up hope! As you move on in your new normal, continue to believe that your prodigal is loved by the Heavenly Father and pray that they will embrace that love. Opportunities to interact with your prodigal should be filled with love and forgiveness. This is a tall order as your relationship is most likely conflicted and you are still walking through healing. But when you get a deep revelation of the Father's love and faithfulness, you will enjoy a freedom that allows you to share that unconditional love. Your trust is not in the prodigal or their love for you. Instead, your trust is in the Lord and His love for you!

My prayer for you

Heavenly Daddy, This is a tall order… to unconditionally love someone who has broken our heart. I ask that You would pour Your anointing oil on this dear reader today. I pray that they will feel Your embrace like never before! Help them fight in the spirit realm with Your weapons of warfare so that they will see the amazing advancements of Your Kingdom in the physical realm. I ask that You would be their Strength when they feel weak, their Hope when they feel hopeless, and their Joy when life tries to drag them down. Thank You that You are a Faithful God and Dad! In Jesus' Name, Amen!

Activation and Application

Read:

- Luke 6:27-38
- I Corinthians 13:1-8a, 13
- II Corinthians 10:3-5

Consider:

- What does unconditional love look like in day-to-day interactions?
- What does unconditional love look like in the midst of conflict?
- What mental cue can I set in place to maintain grace when interactions are difficult?

Declaration:

Dear Lord, I do trust You and Your love for me! Help me to show that love when all I want to do is return pain for pain. I cannot love others unconditionally without Your love flowing through me. Fill me with Your love, I ask, that I might be a reflection of Your heart to each person in my life. Help me to stand strong and move forward in healing and pursuing healthy relationships. Make me more like You, I pray! Thank You, Jesus! Amen.

11

The Homebound Heart: The Repentant Prodigal

"God will give you beauty for ashes, but you have to be willing to give up your ashes."[11]
- Joyce Meyer.

Did you ever run away from home as a child? Maybe you grabbed your backpack, threw in your favorite toy, a jacket, and some snacks before heading to the woods behind your house. At first, you reveled in your newfound freedom! You could go where you wanted, eat what you wanted, and nobody could make you do what you didn't feel like doing. You were your own boss!

But eventually, the urgency that led you to make that choice faded and you began to debate about when and how to return home again.

That might seem to be a simple choice but it is much more complex for a prodigal. A repentant heart is a powerful beginning, but it truly is just the beginning of the journey of restoration and healing. The myriad of emotions the prodigal is struggling with may cause them to head towards home one moment just to turn back around three steps later.

Put yourself in their shoes for a moment. Think about a time when you've made some poor choices that hurt others. Maybe those choices weren't as traumatic, but we've all hurt others at some point in our lives. Pride, anger, frustration, fear… all will wage war against the need to make wrongs right again. The repentant prodigal has much to contend with as they consider returning to home, family, and responsibilities. Consider these:

- **Guilt:** A prodigal is well aware that their choices have caused pain. All the excuses they've thrown out during their time in the "far country" begin to pale in the face of reality. There comes a time when we all must face our failures. Since, most prodigals have annihilated their support network, facing these failures alone can feel very intimidating!
- **Fear:** No one enjoys rejection. The prodigal must consider possible rejection from family, friends, children, previous employers (if a job is needed), and yes, even the church.
- **Humility:** Admitting wrongs comes easily to very few people.
- **Loss:** A prodigal has lost much, even if it was by their own choices. Their current situation may be tolerable but making a choice to turn towards home may end their current provision. Starting over as a repentant

prodigal may lead to a need for finances, a place to live, and a job… as well as the trust of their loved ones.

- **Anxiety:** When realization hits a prodigal and they "come to their senses," they may feel overwhelmed by the enormity of what lies ahead.

- **Consequences:** During the prodigal's sojourn in the "far country," some choices were made that may have long-lasting effects. Your beloved prodigal may now be dealing with situations involving addiction, debt, romantic entanglements, legal issues, custody concerns, and even disease that hadn't been a problem in the past. These consequences do not disappear just because a prodigal decides to turn back to the Lord, their family, and their commitments. The prodigal's new normal includes dealing with those consequences!

Yet, despite all of this, our precious loved one has made a decision! They stood up out of the muck, tossed the last of the slop to the pigs, and jumped over the fence pointing their feet towards home!

What once was lost, now is found!

Suddenly! Your world begins to right itself! Your prodigal has turned his or her heart towards restoration! The sun seems to shine a bit brighter and water tastes sweeter. This time is exciting, yet daunting. Navigating these waters will take some wise guidance, patience, and lots of grace.

Remember the Father in the parable? When he saw his son a long way off, he had compassion on him, ran to him, and hugged him! What love we see demonstrated in that response! A love that, quite honestly, is not so easily replicated in our humanity. The truth of the matter is that when love and trust have been violated we instinctively want to throw our hands over our hearts to protect ourselves from further pain. God knows this and generously provides His grace and compassion to make up the difference for our humanity. Our response to the prodigal can and should be one of embracing love.

I can almost feel some readers saying, "Wait, what about how they stole from me, or lied to me, or cheated on me." You're right! What about that? There are no excuses for their behavior beyond the deception that they've functioned under. We have a decision to make. It's not just about the prodigal returning to the Father's love, it's also about welcoming the prodigal home and being part of that restoration process.

It's necessary that we understand and accept the idea that it's not the prodigal's responsibility to make us feel better or make our pain go away. It is incredibly vital that you find acceptance, love, healing, and strength in your relationship with the Lord. He is your Healer, Deliverer, and Lover of your soul. All you need is found in Him! This prodigal that you've continually brought before Heaven needs to discover this too. In pursuing God, you take the pressure off the prodigal to be your everything and simultaneously give them an example of where to find their healing and deliverance!

Boundaries

There will always be reasons to reject the prodigal or simply keep them an arm's length away. What will you choose to do when the prodigal lands on your doorstep? No one can answer this question for you. Each prodigal situation comes with its own set of circumstances. It's vitally important that you pursue God's Word for your unique situation. Don't wait until you hear that knock on the door to ask Him for instructions! If you've been praying, believing, hoping that your prodigal will come home, then mentally prepare like he or she is coming any day!

Clearly, there are situations when prodigals can be welcomed into the heart but not necessarily the home. If this is the case for you, then consider how you can demonstrate the unconditional "I love you just because of who you are" love to the prodigal. Can he or she eat a daily meal with you? Will they be invited to attend events with you? Would it be possible for an extended family member to house him or her?

If there is a history of any type of abuse, clear boundaries need to be outlined until trust is rebuilt. This is an imperative discussion to have; however, it can be done in gentleness and love. If addiction is involved, a different type of discussion must be had. Though these conversations are crucial, they don't have to happen the first time you sit together. Spend those initial moments emotionally embracing the prodigal! You may not run to the prodigal with arms open wide; but your very facial expression, tone, and demeanor can exclaim, "Welcome home, my loved prodigal! Let's do this together!" This type of attitude will go a long way toward setting the stage for success.

Words to the Wise

Other books have been written focused on aiding the healing and restoration of wounded relationships. Each journey towards healing is different. What works for one situation may backfire in another. However, these nuggets of wise counsel will benefit you as you launch into this unique journey.

- **Daily tap into your Heavenly Father!** In case I haven't reiterated this enough… He is your source and resource! Whether you're headed for a hairpin curve or a relaxing straightaway, His whispered direction will give you what you need! When in doubt as to what action to take, default to His lovingkindness. James 1:5, Hebrews 4:12, John 14:26

- **Build a network of support.** Spend time with others who will encourage you and will also welcome home your prodigal with loving arms. Create opportunities for positive and fun interaction such as game nights, putt-putt golf outings, sports events, or amusement parks. It may take your prodigal some time to feel comfortable joining in, so be sensitive to his or her new normal as well. Be inclusive and encouraging. Building new memories helps heal wounds and develop forward momentum. Proverbs 17:17, Matthew 25: 37-40

- **Think before you speak!** Heart-hurts take a while to heal and when wounds get poked, we are tempted to say things that are more destructive than constructive to the healing process. When you're tempted to lash out… pause, breathe, pray. Consider your motivation in saying what's on your mind. Will it promote healing? Or will it just make you feel vindicated or heard? Can it be said in lovingkindness? Or will it stir up condemnation and guilt? There is much to be considered regarding communication when you are walking through restoration. "Just let it all hang out" is not the best policy! Proverbs 16:32, Proverbs 19:11

- **Leave forgiven deeds in the past!** When you drive down the road, you cannot spend all your time looking in the rearview mirrors or you will crash! The same applies to your restoration journey. Those mirrors are needed at times, but your eyes need to be looking forward. If you've forgiven the pain of the past, then bringing it up will only reopen old wounds and hinder healing. I'm not suggesting that the past never needs to be addressed. However, once forgiveness has been requested, rehashing the painful past will be akin to one step forward, two steps back. II Corinthians 5:17, Philippians 3:13-15, Isaiah 43:18-19

- **Stay positive!** Life is filled with ups and downs no matter which stage you're in! If today is a no-good, rotten, frustrating day, then remember that the sun rises again tomorrow and you can start fresh! His mercies are new every morning and His faithfulness is great! Ask the Lord for a fresh dose of grace each day! Offer that same "Let's start over tomorrow" grace to your family members too! Lamentations 3:22-24

- **Avoid the temptation to manipulate.** When someone has wounded us, they are struggling with their own sense of guilt. It might be easy to take advantage of this to get our own way in any given situation. However, manipulating is not only self-seeking, but it's also a failure to trust God to act on our behalf. Ask the Lord to help you see when your actions lean in that direction. Philippians 2:1-4
- **Keep your trust focused on the One who will never fail!** Trust in the Lord's faithfulness and love for you! Building trust with your beloved prodigal takes time and effort. Your prodigal may feel reluctant to be held accountable on a consistent basis. Trying to police him or her will not strengthen your relationship. This is why your focus needs to be on the Lord! Believe that the Lord is for you, for your family, and for your prodigal. Continue to lay your prodigal at His feet asking the Lord to draw them with His love. Jeremiah 17:7-8, Romans 8:28

NOTE: Do not underestimate the value of a counselor during this season! You have much to wade through and deep hurts to negotiate. Working with a trained counselor will help you sort through ways to handle painful memories, trust issues, and guilt struggles. He or she may also suggest strategies for building a stronger relationship and making new memories. Your healing is the focus of this counseling; however, sessions with the prodigal or other family members may also be beneficial. I highly recommend finding a counselor who understands the value of biblical wisdom and principles. Proverbs 1:1-7

Living purposefully by pursuing wholeness is a valuable and profitable goal. It may seem daunting and even overwhelming, but ultimately, what you gain will far outweigh the painful parts! When a prodigal turns his or her heart towards home, all of Heaven rejoices! And you, my sweet reader, will never regret being part of the redemptive process! As you lay down the past and the pain and choose the forgiveness and restoration, watch God do a work beyond what you imagined! His joy in redemption far exceeds your own; but your role in that joy blesses Your Heavenly Daddy's heart!

My prayer for you

Dear Father, the return of a prodigal is joyous but overwhelming for each person involved. But You are an incredible Guide through this journey! I pray for daily doses of love and wisdom for this precious reader! I ask that You would help them forget what is behind and press on towards this calling. Lift their vision higher, heal their hurting heart, guard their mind against the whispers of the enemy, I pray. Lord, I ask that the healing process for this family would be sealed and complete in the name of Jesus! Thank You, Lord, Amen!

Activation and Application

Read:
- Isaiah 58:6-12
- Ephesians 3:14-21

Consider:

- Reflect on a time that your choices were leading you away from the Father instead of to Him. What caused you to turn and choose a relationship with Him over self-indulgence?
- If your prodigal called today, what words of encouragement would you offer?
- Choose a verse about God's lovingkindness and commit it to memory. (Consider Psalm 143:8)

Declaration:

Dear Lord, I come before You knowing that I need You every step of the way! You have everything I need. Help me to come to You when I am wounded and frustrated. Help me to know when to speak and when to be quiet. I pray that You would enable me to forgive when I need to, forget when I need to, encourage when I need to, and love all the time. I trust You, Lord, and I thank You for forgiving me and meeting my needs. I love You!

12

The Heartbeat of God: Filling the Gap

"We are more than the hands and feet of Jesus; we are His heart extended, offering hope to a hurting world."
- Joy Morey

One of my favorite visuals of God's heart for His children is that of the Cross as a bridge. God's Holiness would not allow for sin in His presence, but to be separated from His children eternally was not an option! So, before Adam was formed, before sin was conceived, before the very foundations of the world were established, God designed a plan. This plan allowed His Very Essence to be capsulized in a flesh and blood man so that through the sacrifice of blood, Perfect Blood, we could be redeemed to Himself! God chose to bridge the gap between His Holiness and our fallen nature with the Cross of Jesus! How the Father loves us! His heartbeat calls to each of His children, "Come home, come home,

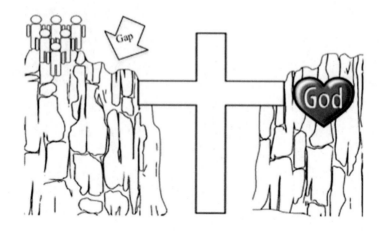

Visual of Jesus' work on the cross bridging the gap between humanity and God's holiness. Note the man-made gap that believers are called to fill!

Yet, a gap remains! Not by God's design but by man's failure to acknowledge our need of the Cross. Or maybe, it's man's inability to grasp how a Holy God can see us in our messiness and still love us. The significance of the gap is the same for each person: separation from the presence of our loving Father and failure to embrace His grace and love. However, the cause of the gap differs from person to person. This gap may be a result of ignorance, disillusionment, fear, pride, selfish desires, or distrust. All are forms of deception.

But, for such a time as this, a time when so many have chosen to run from God instead of to Him, He is raising you and I up to be gap-fillers! Scripture gives us examples of gap-fillers that have gone before us:

- Abraham said, "Here I am," when God chose to test his faith. (Genesis 22)
- Jacob said, "Here I am," when God wanted to give him instruction in a dream. (Genesis 31)

- Moses said, "Here I am," when God was ready to give him an assignment. (Exodus 3)
- Samuel said, "Here I am," when God intended to download a prophecy. (I Samuel 3)
- Isaiah said, "Here I am," when God was recruiting ambassadors. (Isaiah 6)
- Ananias said, "Here I am," when God wanted to launch Paul's ministry (Acts 9)
- Jesus said, "Here I am," when God unfolded His plan of redemption (Psalm 40, Hebrews 10)

What is it that God wants to do… right now… through you? How will you respond?

Will "Here I am!" be your reply?

God has a purpose and a plan He is calling us to enact! This plan starts close to home but expands out to the ends of the earth! He desires that the Gospel (good news!) of His Kingdom be preached to every nation on earth!

Preached? I'm not called to be a preacher. I'm guessing you may not be either. The gift of preaching has not been given to everyone. So, what is it, really, that God wants us to do?

Testify! He wants us to tell of His goodness, to declare His good works in your life! When we testify, we present evidence of God's faithfulness. Sometimes that testimony is in words, but more often than not, our testimony should be living out the truth of who God is and who we are as His children. Our very lives should shout that the Kingdom of God is here and a vibrant part of our daily lives. The deepest revelation of the Kingdom of God is the unsurpassable, unending, unconditional love of the King! When we find ourselves securely entrenched in His love, nothing can rock our world! And, nothing can stop us from extending that love to others in the world around us.

Living out that love is how we become a gap-filler!

Our prodigal is a close-to-home reminder that the world is filled with hurting people. People who have a plan and purpose in this world. People who are unique, ingenious creations that God loves with His Whole Being. Broken, hurting people are everywhere. Some are easier to spot than others. Too easily we assume that the needy people must be the homeless ones, the cross-dressers, the promiscuous. But broken-hearted, life-weary people are all around us. They look like the cashier at the corner bodega. They look like the teacher in your child's classroom. They look like your smiling neighbor down the street. They look like the professional in line at the coffee shop.

You don't know who may need you to be a gap-filler! But God knows! In walking hand-in-hand with our Heavenly Father, we can "tune-in" to His leading as we encounter love-hungry people every day. To truly be a gap-filler, we need to be confident of God's love for us AND confident that He loves others the same, regardless of what they look like or how they live their lives. This knowledge flies in the face of religious thinking. It underscores the truth that God loves us not because of what we do (performance based) but because of who we are (existence based).

If you are struggling with that thought, please take some time to dig into the Word of God and discover for yourself the depth of God's love for ALL people! Follow in the footsteps of Jesus throughout the Gospels and hear the joy in His voice as He interacts with people from all walks of life. Hear the disappointment in His voice when the religious people of His day condemn His compassion. Hear the passion in John's voice when he declares, "God is love!" It's not just what God does… It's WHO HE IS!

The Psalmist said, *"The* LORD *has appeared of old to me, saying: 'Yes, I have loved you with an everlasting love; therefore, with loving-kindness I have drawn you.'"* God loves you, and those around you, with an everlasting, mind-blowing, unstoppable love! He drew you to Himself with loving-kindness. Be a gap-filler by allowing His loving-kindness to pour through your words and actions to those who you encounter in this hurting, love-hungry world! Join your heartbeat to the Father's, "Come home, come home, come home!" May our prayer be that all the lost, broken, lonely, wounded hearts come home to the Father!

My prayer for you

Dearest Daddy! I pray that this precious reader would have a powerful encounter with Your deep, abiding, never-ending love! I ask that You'd reveal Yourself to them in a new and deeper way than ever before! Let them know how much You not only love them, but like who You created them to be. May Your love fill up all the lonely and aching places in their life so that they can effectively pour that love out on others. May Your loving-kindness be tangible to them today. Help this reader to embrace the knowledge that Your love is not because of what they do, but because of who they are, a child made in Your image! Thank You, Father, for Your merciful grace!

Activation and Application

Read:

- I John 4:7-21
- II Timothy 1:7
- Matthew 22:37-39

Consider:

- Think about God's faithfulness to you in the last month. Based on your experience, what words of encouragement can you offer to a friend going through a difficult time?
- What strengths and gifts do you have that you can use to show the love of Jesus? (Maybe buy someone lunch, change someone's oil, babysit for an evening, or help someone create a resume?)
- Imagine someone asked you why you trust God. Prepare a 3 minute testimony about God's faithfulness.

Declaration:

Dear Father God, Thank You for loving me deeply and completely. Thank You for looking beyond the mess of my heart and life and giving me the grace to believe that You are for me, not against me! Thank You that Your perfect love can abolish all fear in my heart and life. I pray that You would help me to look to You when I'm fearful and declare Your faithfulness. Help me to be a conduit of Your lovingkindness to everyone I encounter! I can't do it alone! But I can demonstrate love through Your Holy Spirit as I confidently trust in Your love for me. I want to be a Gap-filler for Your Kingdom! I submit myself to Your plan and purposes. Thank You, Jesus! Amen

13

The Hesitant Heart:
A Letter of Hope for the Precious Prodigal

"Your mistakes don't define your character. It's what you do after you have made the mistake that makes all the difference."[12]
- David Willis

Dearest Wandering One,

Could it be, my precious reader, that you are the prodigal? Have you known relationship and love but wandered away in pursuit of something you thought would be awesome?

But it wasn't quite what you'd expected it would be, was it?

You've been deceived.

You're not alone! There's a reason that Jesus called Satan a father of lies.[a] He has led and will continue to lead many astray because that's all he knows how to do. There is no truth in him… yet he is good at masquerading as "just what we need or want."[b] It's embarrassing when we've been duped, but that's not a reason to stay away from God's loving, hungry arms.

It's not too late; in fact, it's never too late as long as there's breath in your body! God LOVES you and there's nothing you can do to change that truth! Even in all our messiness, He pursues us and longs to lift us out of all the junk.

But He needs our permission. For God to move on your behalf, He needs your cooperation. How? Simply put… ask Him![c] Spill your guts out in sweet surrender! Things got messed up… you know it and He knows it. Ask Him to intervene on your behalf and make a way for your path to collide with His plan for you. Despite all that you've been through, the things you've done and said, the choices you've made, God is still committed to your destiny. The question is, are you?

Finding your way back to the Father is a matter of turning your heart toward "home" by embracing His love as well as asking for and accepting His forgiveness. You can do that right where you are at this very moment. The instant you lay your mistakes down at His feet, you are free from the condemnation of sin and poor choices! When you do that, all of Heaven celebrates that a loved child has come home![d] (I'm grinning just thinking about it!) Imagine your Heavenly Father grabbing you in a bear hug and hollering in your ear, "Welcome home; I've missed you!" Turning your heart toward His love sets you on the course of your destiny. How the Father rejoices!

But I must be real with you. Finding your way back to your loved ones may be more difficult. There are consequences to our choices. Your loved ones may be struggling with hurt, abandonment, resentment, or distrust. Not everyone will be ready to extend forgiveness. Remember, you cannot control them or their choices… you can only control how you act and react to them. You will need to be steady, strong, and forgiving too.

Don't try to navigate this pathway alone. Find support in a pastor, counselor, or trustworthy friend. This is a journey worth traveling even with all the bumps and curves along the way. You will find peace and rest for your soul.ᵉ

*"You don't have to see the whole staircase, just take a step."*¹³
- Martin Luther King Jr.

My prayer for you

Dearest Father! Thank You for loving this dear prodigal unconditionally! You've waited and longed to wrap them in Your loving arms once again! Thank You for forgiveness that we don't deserve. As we lay down our sinful ways and pick up Your robe of righteousness, You enable us to do all things through Your Son, Jesus, who strengthens us! Give this reader the strength they need for the journey of healing ahead. In the name of Jesus, Amen!

Activation and Application

Read:

- Read or re-read chapter two: The Heart of the Father and embrace God's amazing love for you!
- Hide Philippians 4:13 in your heart.

Consider:

- Who can I call on to help me navigate my journey back to the Father?
- What Scriptures from this chapter can I commit to memory to help me stay focused on God's love and faithfulness even in the tough times?
- When it comes to praying, you may feel uncomfortable or rusty or just lost as to how you should do so. Let me encourage you… you cannot go wrong praying the Scriptures! Find verses that speak to your heart and declare them to the Lord. Below is a declaration you can pray as you move forward in faith!

Declaration:

Dear Lord, I'm amazed at how You love me even though I've messed up! Thank You that You never gave up on me! I lay down all my sin and shame at Your feet and believe that Your Word is true, You wipe away all the wrongs I've done. Please help me as I start this journey to live like Your child. Help me to accept Your love and believe that You do have great plans for me. Help me to make things right with my loved ones. Show me Your path to healing and help me follow it even during the difficult times. I know that with You, I'm never alone. Please open my life and heart to trustworthy people who will encourage me. Thank You, Heavenly Father! Amen!

[a] John 8:44
[b] II Cor. 11:14
[c] Matt. 7:7-12
[d] Luke 15:10
[e] Matt. 11:29

Appendix I: Music Resources

Music is a powerful way to lift your heart and encourage your soul and spirit! Worship can get you through the hardest times in your life! It will shift your focus from the problems in your life to the Problem Solver! There are literally millions of wonderful songs available. Here are some that I have found encouraging and healing.

Start building your faith! Listen to Brandon Lake, Dante Bowe, and Josh Baldwin sing "Too Good to Not Believe."

Chapter 1: *The Hopeful Heart: Dealing with Relational Trauma*
- For King and Country: Busted Heart (Hold On To Me)
- Manafest: Never Let You Go
- Tauren Wells: God's Not Done With You

Chapter 2: *The Heart of the Father: Unending Love*
- Britt Nicole: Through Your Eyes
- Jesus Culture: (Your Love is) Fierce
- TobyMac: Made to Love

Chapter 3: *The Heart of the Prodigal: Ripe for Deception*
- Nine Lashes: Heartbeats
- Jordan Feliz: Beloved

Chapter 4: *The Hurting Heart: Choosing to Forgive*
- Matthew West: Forgiveness
- Mercy Me: Even If

Chapter 5: *The Heart for the Prodigal: Taking a Stand*
- Warr Acres: Hope Will Rise
- Red Rocks Worship: Your Love Changes Everything
- Champion: Dante Bowe

Chapter 6: *The Humble Heart: Accepting Responsibility*
- Group 1 Crew: Little Closer
- For King and Country: Fix My Eyes

Chapter 7: *The Hungry Heart: Pursuing Relationship*
- Jonny Diaz: Breathe
- Kari Jobe: Speak to Me

Chapter 8: *The Healing Heart: The Productive Process*
- Kari Jobe: Healer
- Casting Crowns: Just Be Held
- Rita Springer: Defender

Chapter 9: *The Heart with Vision: Speaking Life*
- TobyMac: Speak Life
- Hillsong: Say the Word

Chapter 10: *The Heart of Restoration: New but Purposeful Normal*
- Leanna Crawford: Truth I'm Standing On
- Unspoken: Good Fight

Chapter 11: *The Homebound Heart: The Repentant Prodigal*
- TobyMac: Beyond Me
- Unspoken: The Cure

Chapter 12: *The Heartbeat of God: Filling the Gap*
- Newsboys: Love Riot
- For King and Country: Proof of Your Love

Chapter 13: *The Hesitant Heart: A Letter of Hope for the Precious Prodigal*
- Hawk Nelson: Drops in the Ocean
- Jordan Feliz: Never Too Far Gone
- Crowder: Forgiven
- TobyMac: Scars

Note: These songs are easily accessible through youtube.com or other music streaming services. I don't own the rights to any of these songs.

Appendix II: Helpful Links

Marriage and Family Support:

- Rejoice Marriage Ministries, https://www.rejoiceministries.org/
- Focus on the Family: https://www.focusonthefamily.com/
- Chris & Cindy Beall: https://www.familylife.com/podcast/guest/chris-and-cindy-beall/
- Stormie Omartian: https://www.stormieomartian.com/

Addiction Recovery:

- Celebrate Recovery, A Christ-Centered 12 Step Program: https://www.celebraterecovery.com/
- Adult & Teen Challenge: https://teenchallengeusa.org/

Missing Persons:

- National Center for Missing and Exploited Children: https://www.missingkids.org/search
- Global Missing Children Network: https://globalmissingkids.org/
- United States Department of Justice: https://www.justice.gov/actioncenter/report-and-identify-missing-persons

Prayer Hotlines:

- https://justdisciple.com/christian-prayer-hotline/
- Trinity Broadcasting Network 24/7 Prayer line: 714-731-1000
- 700 Club Prayer Line: 1-800-700-7000

Acknowledgements

With an overflowing heart, I give thanks to my Daddy King who has shown Himself strong on my behalf. You are the Lover of my soul and the Keeper of my heart! I continue to say, "Yes and amen!" to Your promises.

Thank you to my sweet husband, Andy! You have stood by me, encouraged me, and celebrated each step of the process. Love you forever!

Caleb and Miranda, thank you for having grace with your mom when I'm so engrossed in the process that I miss what you're saying to me! You are my favorite(s)!

It is a powerful thing to be raised in the Truth of God's Word. I honor my own parents, Dave & Judy, as well as Andy's parents, Dave and Ann. Thank you for introducing us to the Savior of our souls!

Eric & Sarah… pastors, co-servers, and precious friends! I am so thankful for your friendship, wisdom, leadership, and support. Let's do another 20 years together!

Every woman needs her squad! I'm ever so thankful for mine! Kenitra & Kim, Thank you for sharing laughter, tears, snacks, silliness, wisdom, shopping, dreams, and memories with me. I love us!

So many people have been part of our journey as a couple. You don't go through 3+ decades of marriage without some ups and downs. Andy and I are thankful for the godly couples that He has placed in our lives. There are too many to name, but I suspect you know who you are!

Thanks to my dynamic editing duo: Ciera Lehmann and Miranda Morey. Your attention to detail and insight are a blessing!

Finally, to those who have encouraged me in the writing of this book, offered input and wisdom, helped me navigate the process, and are even now praying for those who read it, I am deeply appreciative of your investment!

Endnotes

1. Eller, Suzanne. 2014. *The Mended Heart: God's Healing for Your Broken Places*, Revell
2. Liddell, Eric. 1985. *The Disciplines of the Christian Life*. Epiphany Books.(London: Society for Promoting Christian Knowledge, 1985), 121–122.
3. Hazlett, Bob. 2015. *Think Like Heaven: Change Your Thinking, Change Your World*, Whittaker House
4. Ziglar, Zig. 1997. *Over the Top*, Thomas Nelson Inc, 1997 ISBN: 9781418530280
5. Vallotton, Kris. 2019. "5 Lies That Will Keep You Trapped in Unforgiveness." *Kris Vallotton* (blog), September 6, 2019. https://www.krisvallotton.com/5-lies-that-will-keep-y ou-trapped-in-unforgiveness?fbclid=IwAR0tQNiQJsc- spn_QAIs9Bqh1dFv2LMN4tM-M87JbBFNCMz8FbRi- 3woEWq0U
6. Voskamp, Ann. 2015. "Ann Voskamp's Facebook Page" Facebook, November 3, 2015. https:// www.facebook.com/324577877554393/photos /a.369461463066034/1083256945019812
7. Willis, Dave. 2013. "4 Things God Wants You to Remember When Life is Hard." *Patheos* (blog), May 7, 2013. https://www.patheos.com/blogs/davewillis/4-things-to-re member-when-life-is-hard/
8. Caine, Christine 2015. "Christine Caine's Facebook Page" Facebook, November 12, 2015.https:// www.facebook.com/143678730088/photos /a.10150570623045089/10156334843195089
9. Lehmann, Eric. 2020. Freedom Church, Wesley Chapel, Florida. Sermon Series entitled: *Develop Your Imagination*, January-March 2020
10. Chapman, Gary. 2009. *The Five Love Languages Singles Edition*, Northfields Publishing

11. Meyer, Joyce. "The Great Exchange." Uploaded on November 26, 2019. YouTube video, .43 min. https://www.facebook.com/joycemeyerministries/videos/573146300100228/
12. Willis, David (@*Davewillis*). 2016. "Dave Willis Twitter Post" Twitter, July 16, 2016, 4:51 p.m. https://twitter.com/davewillis/status/754418255998160896.
13. Attributed to Martin Luther King, Jr. by Marian Wright Edelman. 1988, *And Still We Rise: Interviews With 50 Black Role Models*, Edited by Barbara A. Reynolds, Chapter: Children's Advocate – Marian Wright Edelman, Start Page 73, Quote Page 74 and 75, USA Today Books: Gannett Co. Inc., Washington D.C.

Contact the Author

Thank you so much for reading *The Missing Ones: A Journey of Hope and Healing for Families of Prodigals!* If you have been blessed by this book, Joy would love to hear from you. Please email her at ...

TheMissingOnes@DiscoveringJoy.net

Or check out her website: www.DiscoveringJoy.net